GOSPEL FOUNDATIONS®

The Coming Rescue

| VOL. 4 | 2 KINGS – MALACHI |

LifeWay Press® • Nashville, Tennessee

From the creators of *The Gospel Project*, Gospel Foundations is a six-volume resource that teaches the storyline of Scripture. It is comprehensive in scope yet concise enough to be completed in just one year. Each seven-session volume includes videos to help your group understand the way each text fits into the storyline of the Bible.

© 2018 LifeWay Press® • Reprinted 2019

ISBN 978-1-5359-0361-5 • Item 005803635

Dewey decimal classification: 230
Subject headings: CHRISTIANITY / GOSPEL / SALVATION

EDITORIAL TEAM

Michael Kelley
Director, Discipleship and Groups Ministry

Brian Dembowczyk
Managing Editor

Joel Polk
Editorial Team Leader

Daniel Davis, Josh Hayes
Content Editors

Brian Daniel
Manager, Short-Term Discipleship

Darin Clark
Art Director

We believe that the Bible has God for its author; salvation for its end; and truth, without any mixture of error, for its matter and that all Scripture is totally true and trustworthy. To review LifeWay's doctrinal guideline, please visit lifeway.com/doctrinalguideline.

Scripture quotations are taken from the Christian Standard Bible®, Copyright © 2017 by Holman Bible Publishers. Used by permission. Christian Standard Bible® and CSB® are federally registered trademarks of Holman Bible Publishers.

To order additional copies of this resource, write to LifeWay Resources Customer Service; One LifeWay Plaza; Nashville, TN 37234; fax 615-251-5933; call toll free 800-458-2772; order online at LifeWay.com; email orderentry@lifeway.com; or visit the LifeWay Christian Store serving you.

Printed in the United States of America

Groups Ministry Publishing • LifeWay Resources
One LifeWay Plaza • Nashville, TN 37234

Contents

About *The Gospel Project*

Gospel Foundations is from the creators of *The Gospel Project*, which exists to point kids, students, and adults to the gospel of Jesus Christ through weekly group Bible studies and additional resources that show how God's plan of redemption unfolds throughout Scripture and still today, compelling them to join the mission of God.

The Gospel Project provides theological yet practical, age-appropriate Bible studies that immerse your entire church in the story of the gospel, helping to develop a gospel culture that leads to gospel mission.

Gospel Story

Immersing people of all ages in the storyline of Scripture: God's plan to rescue and redeem His creation through His Son, Jesus Christ.

Gospel Culture

Inspiring communities where the gospel saturates our experience and doubters become believers who become declarers of the gospel.

Gospel Mission

Empowering believers to live on mission, declaring the good news of the gospel in word and deed.

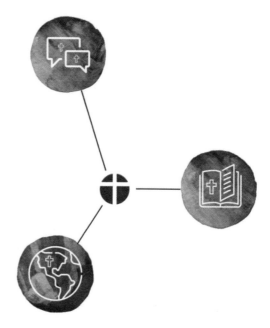

How to Use This Study

This Bible-study book includes seven weeks of content for group and personal study.

Group Study

Regardless of what day of the week your group meets, each week of content begins with the group session. Each group session uses the following format to facilitate simple yet meaningful interaction among group members and with God's Word.

Introducing the Study & Setting the Context
These pages include **content and questions** to get the conversation started and **infographics** to help group members see the flow of the biblical storyline.

Continuing the Discussion
Each session has a corresponding **teaching video** to help tell the Bible story. These videos have been created specifically to challenge the group to consider the entire story of the Bible. After watching the video, continue the **group discussion** by reading the Scripture passages and discussing the questions on these pages. Finally, conclude each group session with **a personal missional response** based on what God has said through His Word.

Personal Study

Three personal studies are provided for each session to take individuals deeper into Scripture and to supplement the content introduced in the group study. With **biblical teaching and introspective questions**, these sections challenge individuals to grow in their understanding of God's Word and to respond in faith.

Leader Guide

A tear-out leader guide for each session is provided on pages 95-108, which includes possible answers to questions highlighted with an icon and suggestions for various sections of the group study.

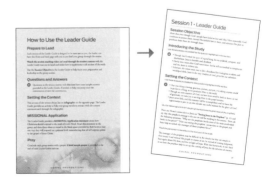

God's Word to You

Hope in the Midst of Darkness

God's plan to redeem humanity centered on Him forming a people through whom He would bring blessing to the world (Gen. 12:1-3). It would be through this people—the descendants of Abraham—that One would come to crush the head of the serpent (Gen. 3:15) and put an end to sin and death. Not only would God's blessing come through the Israelites, it would be extended to them. God had promised to care for His people, to protect them, and to be their God and their Father.

But one of the ways good fathers bless is by disciplining their wayward, disobedient children. Just as God had promised to take care of Israel many times, he had also warned them of the consequences of their disobedience. But they failed to listen. Time and time again, they played the harlot with pagan gods, wanting the faithful blessings of the one true God without being faithful to Him.

God's response is found in the prophets and can be summarized by one word: *Repent*. God called on His people to turn from their wicked ways and turn back to Him. If they did, He would receive them back, but if they did not, He would bring destruction upon them—not punitive destruction but restorative destruction. His discipline is always corrective.

And still, the people would not listen; they would not repent. So judgment came. First, it came in the form of the Assyrian army, which conquered the Northern Kingdom of Israel and hauled off its people into captivity. But even witnessing this did not draw the rest of God's people to repentance. And so, judgment came again, this time through the Babylonian army, which destroyed the Southern Kingdom of Judah, including Jerusalem, and exiled its people.

These were dark days for God's people. They were prisoners in foreign lands, their land was occupied by a pagan people, and the temple lay in ruins. The blessings of God seemed more distant than ever. Impossible even. But even if it was difficult for the people to see, God was drawing His master plan together—the promised Seed, the Deliverer, was closer than ever. In a blistering cadence of activity to close out the Old Testament, God restored His people to the land and the temple and city of Jerusalem were rebuilt, but then God went silent. For four hundred years, the people looked, listened, and waited—the stage was set for Jesus to come and crush the serpent's head.

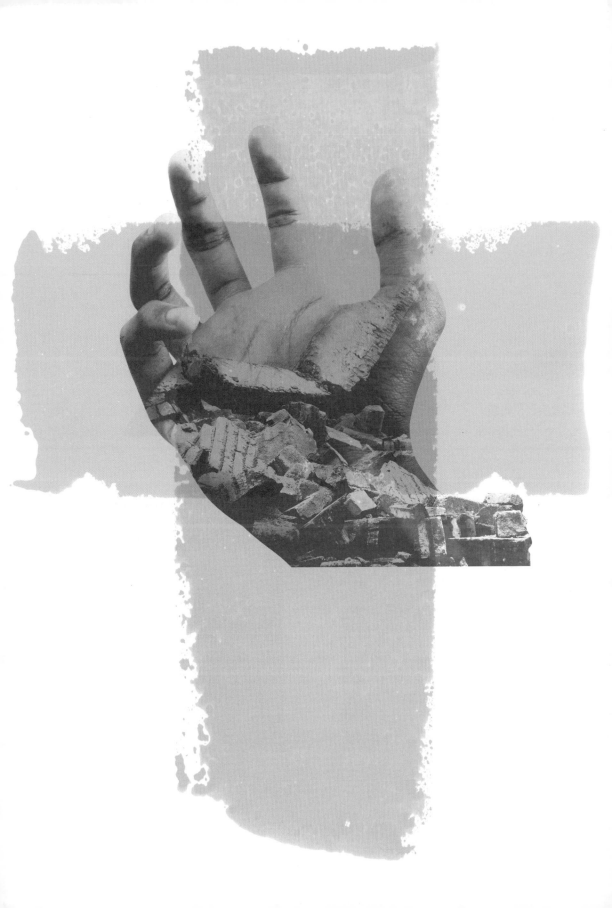

God's Faithful Love

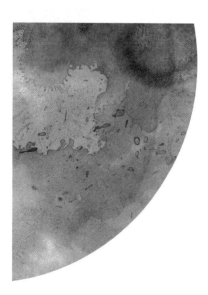

Introducing the Study

The people of God had longed for a king to be like the other nations, but God knew their request was a rejection of Him as their true King. Nevertheless, He gave His people what they asked for, and though there were high points in the reigns of Saul, David, and Solomon, each one proved in different ways that the only true, just, good king—the king we all really long for—is God Himself.

 Based on your study of these kings, in what ways did their failings reveal that Jesus is the King we all need?

After Solomon, the kingdom of Israel was torn in two, and on the whole, the kings who would follow continued to lead the people of God down the road of idolatry. Eventually, God's promised judgment would come. But God was not willing to abandon His people, despite their unfaithfulness. He sent a string of prophets to deliver His word to His people, warning them of what was to come and urging them to repent and return to Him.

> **When was a time you knew God was pursuing you, even if you were not pursuing or welcoming Him?**

Setting the Context

Solomon was the last king to reign over **the united kingdom** of Israel. Under his son, Rehoboam, the kingdom was torn in two: Israel in the north and Judah in the south. Both nations saw many kings come and go over the next four hundred years. Some of the kings of Judah were faithful, but these godly leaders were rare.

The period of **the divided kingdom** was not marked by faithfulness but faithlessness. The Israelites followed the examples of their kings and slipped deeper and deeper into the worship of foreign gods. God had warned His people of idolatry, that judgment would come if they turned their backs on their relationship with Him, and that's precisely what would happen.

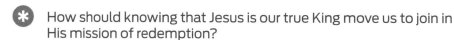 How should knowing that Jesus is our true King move us to join in His mission of redemption?

But before Israel and Judah were taken over by foreign powers, the Lord sent **prophets** to deliver His word—to warn of what was to come and to urge His people to repent and return to Him. Truly His love was unfailing, and the prophet Hosea would demonstrate God's love for His people both powerfully and visibly.

Though these prophets primarily brought warning of God's judgment, they also proclaimed God's message of love and hope. In **"Seeing Jesus in the Prophets"** (p. 11), we see that the rescue God had promised since Adam and Eve was coming closer to fulfillment.

How can warnings be a sign of love and devotion?

✛ CHRIST Connection

Hosea's relationship with Gomer reminds us of God's relationship with the people of Israel and with us. Even though God's people are unfaithful and love other things more than God, God still loves us. It was because of His love that God sent Jesus to die on the cross for our sin and bring us back to Him.

Seeing Jesus *in the* Prophets

Hosea Pursued His Adulterous Wife; Bought Her Back from Slavery for Purity (Hos. 3)	**Jesus** Gave Himself for His Church to Make Her Holy and Blameless (Eph. 5:25-27)
Jonah In the Belly of a Great Fish Three Days and Nights (Jonah 1:17)	**The Better Jonah** In the Heart of the Earth Three Days and Nights (Matt. 12:39-41)
Joel Prophesied of God's Spirit Poured Out on Those Who Call on Yahweh (Joel 2:28-32)	**Jesus** Pours Out His Spirit on All Who Call on Him to Be Saved (Acts 2; Rom. 10)
Jeremiah Prophesied of a New Covenant for the Forgiveness of Sin (Jer. 31:31-34)	**Jesus** Shed His Blood to Establish the Covenant for the Forgiveness of Sin (Matt. 26:28)
Ezekiel Prophesied of a Resurrection for God's People, a Restoration to the Land (Ezek. 37)	**Jesus** The Resurrection and the Life for All Who Believe in Him (John 11:25-26)

Continuing the Discussion

 Watch this session's video, and then continue the group discussion using the following guide.

Does it surprise you that God would command Hosea to do what he did? Why or why not?

Why is Hosea's story both a vivid and appropriate illustration of God's relationship with His people?

As a group, read Hosea 1:2-9.

 How are we like Gomer in our relationship with God, and God like Hosea?

Why is it so easy to live as if the consequences of sin don't apply to us?

What does this reveal about our nature and our relationship with God?

In this real-life analogy, Hosea, the good man, represented the Lord. Gomer, the unfaithful wife, represented ancient Israel. But Gomer also represents each of us, since we too are unfaithful and love many different things besides God. How bad were God's people? Hosea 2 tells of their promiscuity and adultery (2:2), of their shameful behavior in bearing children of promiscuity (2:4-5), and of their pursuit of other lovers (2:5-7).

As a group, read Hosea 2:16-23.

What strikes you the most in this description of God's love and commitment to His people?

 What does this passage teach us about the nature of true love?

How is that different from the love we readily see and experience in our culture?

Hosea's love and commitment to his wife would not depend on her faithfulness, just as God's love for us does not depend on ours. Mercifully, God's love for His people is based in His own steadfast loving character, not in the fickle conduct of people.

As a group, read Hosea 3:1-5.

What is so shocking about Hosea's actions?

How does this remind us of what God has done for us in the gospel?

Gomer had left Hosea, forsaking his love and care for her. But that did not stop Hosea. He sought her out and found her as a slave. Hosea paid the price to purchase her freedom and brought her back to his home as his wife. This is a vivid picture of the gospel. We all were once slaves to sin, and yet, God sought us out and paid the price of His own Son, Jesus, so that we might live in freedom as His own.

MISSIONAL Application

Record in this space at least one way you will apply the truth of Scripture as a sinner saved by the ever-faithful love and grace of the Creator God.

Personal Study 1

God pursues His people though they are an unfaithful bride.

Read Hosea 1:2-9.

What does the Bible mean when it speaks of *prophets*? God's Old Testament prophets were His mouthpieces. They were the ones who stood before the people and with heavenly authority said, "Thus says the LORD." Typically, the messages the prophets shared centered on the people's need to repent of their sins and God's coming judgment if they failed to do so.

In the case of Hosea though, the prophetic role involved more than speaking. God planned for this prophet to share a walking, living, breathing message, not just a verbal one. And this message would require him to marry an unfaithful woman. Hosea was under no pretense about the kind of relationship he was entering into. He knew from the beginning that this marriage would be filled with infidelity and heartache.

God's command was especially jarring because God expected faithfulness in the marriages of His people. But this prophet was not to prophesy against marital unfaithfulness like the prophet Micah. Instead, Hosea was to pursue, marry, and embrace a wife with the full knowledge of her history and even her future.

In fact, if we look through this passage, we see a distinct difference in the way the children who would come into this marriage are described. Notice in verse 3 the language used to describe their first son: "she conceived and bore him a son." But then look down to verses 6 and 8. In both cases, the language has changed: "she conceived and gave birth…"

The shift in language suggests that while the first child was truly the child of Hosea, the second and third children were a result of Gomer's ongoing unfaithfulness. Here, then, we start to see the fullness of God's command to His prophet. He was to marry an unfaithful wife, and he would be reminded for years—even decades—of that unfaithfulness while caring and providing for illegitimate children.

Why did Hosea have to marry Gomer? You see, when God designed marriage, He instituted a relationship of such intimacy, of such sacrifice, of such mutual love, that it would serve as a walking, talking, living, breathing illustration of the relationship between Christ and the church (Eph. 5:32). In commanding Hosea to take an unfaithful wife like Gomer, God was demonstrating the intensely personal relationship that He desires with His people. Further, He illustrated just how painful and sacrificial that relationship has always been on Him, the faithful partner loving the unfaithful one.

We might well wonder what Hosea was feeling as he stood next to Gomer at their wedding ceremony. Perhaps he felt a glimmer of the same thing that God was feeling as He entered into a covenant relationship with Israel. Perhaps he experienced the painful knowledge of what was and what was to come, and yet, he was compelled by love to move forward anyway.

Why was it not sufficient for Hosea to deliver God's message with words alone?

What do you think was most difficult for Hosea in his marriage to Gomer?

How might Hosea's life experience have influenced the way he spoke the word of the Lord?

Personal Study 2

God promises His people He will love them forever.

Read Hosea 2:16-23.

If Hosea, a man, showed this kind of love and faithfulness to his wife, knowing her pattern of unfaithful behavior, then how much more must God love His people? How much more passionately does His affection burn even for those who time and time again walk—and run—away from Him?

This picture of the love of God stands in stark contrast to what passes for love in our culture. Think about it for a second—how trivially do we throw around the word *love*? How many times have you said that word today and with how many different meanings?

We love sports, movies, pets, food, actors, games, and a host of other things. We throw around the word without thinking about it; it's part of our regular vocabulary. It seems to us, at least based on the way we use the word, that love is solely a feeling, an emotion. Therefore, we quickly fall in and out of love with everything from the taste of certain foods to people with whom we are meant to be in a covenant relationship. According to this mind-set, love is not a decision and a commitment but instead rests on the shaky foundation of personal preference and taste.

But with God, we find the true definition of the word *love*. Its definition is forged not with words but with action, exemplified by the work of Jesus on the cross: "Love consists in this: not that we loved God, but that he loved us and sent his Son to be the ~~atoning sacrifice~~ *propitiation* for our sins" (1 John 4:10).

God, in His love, not only pursued us in the midst of our unfaithfulness, as Hosea did with Gomer, but God promises His love to us forever. Threaded inseparably into the narrative of Hosea's marriage is God's promise of love for His own people. Just as Hosea was called to continue to pursue and love his wife, so God had committed Himself to His people.

It's not that love is devoid of emotion when it comes to God—far from it. In fact, these verses, along with a host of others in both the Old and New Testaments, show us the deep affection God has for His people (see Deut. 7:8-9; Isa. 54:8-10; Jer. 31:3; Rom. 8:31-39; 1 John 4:8-11).

God's love is much deeper than that, however. His love, and all true love, involves willing pursuit and necessary sacrifice for the sake of the one being loved. It's important to see in these verses that God is the One doing the pursuing. He is sacrificing; He is leading; He is giving. His people are the ones responding to that initiating love of God. So it is with us.

Like the people of Israel in the days of Hosea, we have joined ourselves to the things of this world. Though God might have chosen to leave such an unfaithful people to our foolish choices, He does not. Instead, He continues to seek and pursue us, initiating the love that exists between Creator and creature, Savior and sinner. We need to be clear: We did not come to God; He came to us, and we respond to His love.

But it's also important to notice in these verses that there is no time limit to the love God is promising. The imagery of eternity is intertwined in this poetic treatment of the love of God. We will be His people forever, resting securely in Him. He has promised and given us love, and that promise and gift will never be revoked.

Which of God's promises in Hosea 2:16-23 stand out to you the most? Why?

Why is it important to know that God will not withdraw His love from His people? How does that help you today?

Personal Study 3

God purchases His people out of slavery.

Read Hosea 3:1-5.

At some point between Hosea 1 and Hosea 3, Gomer left. We don't know exactly why or when she did, or if her leaving was for the first time. Whatever the reason, Gomer had escaped out of the house of Hosea and into slavery.

The imagery is vivid and powerful. Hosea, the jilted and abandoned but faithful husband who had every right to turn his back. Gomer, powerless to affect her situation. And then the husband, in love, paying the price to purchase the freedom of the one he loved. This poignant picture relates to the message of the gospel in several ways.

First, it wasn't just that Gomer was gone; she was enslaved. Because of her lifestyle, Gomer had found herself enslaved and powerless to change her own circumstances. Instead, she was at the mercy of others.

Like Gomer, you and I, apart from Christ, are enslaved to the pattern and ways of this world. We are chained by our own sin, and both because of our nature and our choices, we are incapable of escaping from these bonds. This is sometimes difficult for us to accept because we live in a day when freedom is equated to the lack of restraint.

Ironically, the opposite is actually true. We are enslaved by our own sinful desires and incapable of living in the acceptably righteous fashion required of us. Like Gomer, we are on the slave block, and unless someone intervenes, our eternal destiny is set. We will be chained for all eternity as a result of our sin.

Furthermore, Hosea would have had every right to leave his wife to what she deserved, but he did not. The Lord commanded him to "go" to her because there was no way she could come to him, even if she had wanted to.

But just as Hosea went to Gomer when she was powerless to return to him, so Jesus came to us and freed us. This freedom came not as a result of our efforts, struggling against the chains that kept us in bondage. It came instead from One who loved us enough to come to us, and though we have been unfaithful, He faithfully gave up His life in our place.

Finally, there was a price to be paid. Hosea did not buy back Gomer on emotion, sentiment, or good intentions. He didn't stand at a distance and shout about his love for her; instead, Hosea recognized that freedom doesn't come cheaply, and so he came with his pockets full to pay the price so that the one he loved could go free.

In an even greater way, there was a costly price to be paid for our freedom. As rebellious sinners, God's justice demands death as payment for our rebellion, and that justice must be satisfied. The price to be paid for us was not measured in the weight of silver but in blood. Jesus Himself was the price paid, and because He gave up His own life, we can go free.

This entire process can be summed up in a single word—*redemption*. To redeem something is to buy it back. This is what Hosea did for Gomer, and this what Jesus Christ has done for us at the cross.

In what ways have you found sin to be a snare that enslaves rather than something that frees?

How does this view of sin differ from the world's?

How does understanding the love of Hosea for Gomer help us grow in gratitude for how God has treated us?

God's Continued Pursuit

Introducing the Study

Though God's people had wandered far from Him, led by both their own desires and a series of kings who pulled the nations further into idolatry, God loved His people still. He was like a husband to an unfaithful wife, and to make sure His people knew that, God called Hosea to live it out for all of them to see.

> How did the story of Hosea and Gomer mirror God's relationship with His people?

God loves His people with a love not based on their conduct or faithfulness but instead based on His own unchanging character. Because He loves like this, God is a pursuing God. He will not merely state His love in words; He will actively go after sinners, pursuing them to bring them back into a right relationship with Himself. The prophet Jonah experienced this kind of pursuit—both for himself and for a people who were far from God.

 Why might we struggle with the thought of God pursuing other people, even our enemies, for salvation?

Setting the Context

Jonah, whose name means "dove," was a prophet in the Northern Kingdom of Israel, just as Hosea was. Though most of the information we have about Jonah comes from the book bearing his name, God had previously used Jonah to declare God's grace and coming blessing to Israel (2 Kings 14:25). Soon after Jonah's proclamation, under the leadership of King Jeroboam II, Israel found itself living as richly as they ever had. Unfortunately, this blessing ended up being a stumbling block for God's people. Their prosperity led to national pride. So the Lord raised up other prophets to call on Israel to turn from their arrogance. The nation needed to **repent or face the consequences**.

 Why is the message of "repentance or consequences" applicable for all people at all times?

At the same time, a new nation had risen to power on the world scene. **The Assyrians** were brutal conquerors, and the nations lived in fear of them. This empire would be the target of Jonah's message, as God told him to go to **Nineveh**, a city great in number but also in importance, maybe even a capital in the Assyrian Empire.

But Jonah resisted and only delivered God's message grudgingly. In Jonah we find one reluctant to preach God's word to a particular group of people. We find a messenger who believed he knew God's message better than the One who gave it. And this sets up a confrontation between God and His prophet in which Jonah would learn the truth about **"God's Compassion Toward the Nations"** (p. 23).

How should God's continued pursuit of the nations challenge our worldview?

✝ CHRIST Connection

Jonah was a prophet who rejected God's call, ran away from his enemies, and eventually obeyed God grudgingly. Jesus followed God's call, faced His opponents, and obeyed God joyfully (Heb. 12:2). While we were still sinners, Christ died for us.

God's **Compassion**
Toward the **Nations**

THE NATIONS	GOD'S COMPASSION	THE RESULT
All the Nations of the Earth (Gen. 12; Isa. 49)	God blessed Abraham to be a blessing to the world and raised up His Servant to restore Israel and be a light to the nations	People from every tribe, tongue, people, and nation are blessed through faith in Jesus, Abraham's descendant (Gal. 3:8; Rev. 5:9)
Rahab, a Canaanite Prostitute (Josh. 2; 6)	God granted protection to Rahab and her family from the destruction of Jericho	Rahab became the great-great grandmother of King David and an ancestor of Jesus (Matt. 1:5)
Ruth, a Moabitess (Ruth 1–4)	God provided a husband and family for Ruth from among the Israelites	Ruth became the great-grandmother of King David and an ancestor of Jesus (Matt. 1:5)
Naaman, Commander of the Army of Aram (2 Kings 5)	God healed Naaman of a skin disease through Elisha	Naaman confessed there is no God in the whole world except in Israel (2 Kings 5:15)
The Ninevites (Jonah 1–4)	God sent Jonah to preach against the Ninevites	The Ninevites believed God and repented, and God relented of their destruction (Jonah 3:5-10)

Continuing the Discussion

▶ Watch this session's video, and then continue the group discussion using the following guide.

Jonah is one of the most familiar stories in the Bible. How has your understanding of this story changed over time?

In what ways does the story of Jonah challenge you personally?

As a group, read Jonah 1:1-4,17.

✳ What are some reasons we might run from the call of God?

Can you share a time when you ran from the Lord?

What were some of the means God used to pursue you?

As the Book of Jonah opens, we find a reluctant prophet. Jonah had no misunderstanding of God's message; he also had no misunderstanding of God's character. Jonah didn't run because of fear; as the rest of the book reveals, he ran from God's call because he knew of God's compassion. He knew that if the Ninevites did indeed repent, God would give them what he did not want them to have: forgiveness.

As a group, read Jonah 2:10–3:5,10.

Does the response of the Ninevites surprise you? Why or why not?

✳ What can we learn about evangelism from what happened in Nineveh?

Who is one person in your life that you might deem beyond God's reach? How does this passage encourage you in that relationship?

Jonah's message was simple and straightforward, but it was filled with God's power. This reminds us of the power of God's proclaimed Word, that it goes out and accomplishes its purposes. We should be filled with confidence when we share the Word of God, not because of our own strength as His messengers but because God works in power through His Word.

As a group, read Jonah 4:1-4,8-11.

> Why was Jonah so angry?

> What groups of people could we possibly withhold the gospel from because we do not want them to be saved?

✳ How should our prayers both for ourselves and others change in light of these passages from Jonah?

Jonah felt such animosity toward these people that he asked God to take his life rather than see them be forgiven. We should take this as a warning. We must confront prejudice and bias in our own lives, making sure that we understand our own need of God's unending mercy and grace so that in humility we share the gospel with anyone and everyone we can.

✝ MISSIONAL Application

Record in this space at least one way you will apply the truth of Scripture as a recipient of the grace and compassion of God through faith in Jesus Christ.

Personal Study 1

God pursues a rebellious people and prophet.

Read Jonah 1:1-4,17.

Why in the world would someone think he could run from God? God is not like a man; His reach is boundless and His eyes move throughout the earth. Yet Jonah, despite being a prophet, decided that God's call was so distasteful that he wanted to escape from it. Jonah concluded that he could flee from God's call—indeed from God Himself—if he only ran far enough away.

So Jonah did indeed get up like God told him, but instead of heading straight for Nineveh, he bought a ticket on a ship to get away. Nineveh was to the east of Israel, while the Mediterranean Sea was to the west. Jonah literally went in the other direction. He wanted to be as far away as possible from where God called him to be. But it wasn't the character of the Ninevites that made Jonah want to head the other direction. It wasn't the message of coming judgment either. It was the character of the God who sent him.

Jonah knew God well enough to know that God is gracious, compassionate, and full of mercy. Furthermore, he knew that God was giving the Ninevites a warning, inviting them to repent. Jonah could see how this might play out, even if the chances were slim—the Ninevites might repent, and God would forgive them. And so, Jonah's hatred for the Ninevites led him to hold back from them the message of God.

Like Jonah, we know the character of God. We know that He is quick to forgive, that His compassion and grace extend to all who call on Him. But sometimes we too think of certain people as being unworthy of that grace (as if being worthy were a qualification). And like Jonah, one of the ways we demonstrate our own judgment is by our failure to share the gospel with them.

But just as God was unwilling to give up on the Ninevites, He was also unwilling to give up on Jonah. While Jonah was running from God, God was running after him. God "threw" a mighty storm into the sea that was so terrible that even the hardened sailors suddenly turned very religious. There are no atheists in foxholes, or on ships in a God-sized storm!

Jonah simply could have acknowledged his disobedience and asked the crew to turn around and row for shore. After all, he had resolved to stop running from God (a pointless endeavor anyway). But Jonah, even now, was too full of pride and hatred to bend his will to that of God's. He would rather die. So into the raging waters he went. But God had other ideas. The murky depths of the sea cannot end God's relentless pursuit of those upon whom He has fixed His gaze. God sent a great fish to swallow Jonah and preserve his life, giving him time to consider his next move.

Why do you think Jonah was so reluctant to speak the word of the Lord to the Ninevites?

When have you felt like Jonah, uneasy about what God was calling you to do?

Do you typically see yourself as Jonah in this story or as the Ninevites? Why is it important that we learn from both?

Personal Study 2

God extends mercy to a rebellious people and prophet.

Read Jonah 2:10–3:5,10.

Let's zoom out here for a minute and remind ourselves of what is going on. We have the enemies of God who are staring down God's judgment because of their sins. We have God choosing a messenger to deliver a message of warning so that this people might repent. And we have God's chosen messenger, who was unwilling to bend his will to God's, now sitting in the belly of a fish for three days and three nights.

Apparently, spending a few days in a fish is a fine place to reevaluate your priorities. It served as that kind of environment for Jonah, and we should learn from this. Part of trusting in God's perfect fatherhood is recognizing that as our perfect Father, God exercises the right discipline at the right time in the right way. Discipline is not evidence of God's lack of care; it's the proof of His love.

Ironically, Jonah found himself in the exact same position as the Ninevites. Not in terms of being in a fish but in his disobedience. Jonah was also staring down God's discipline, and he too needed to repent and ask God for forgiveness.

After Jonah's repentance, it is as if the story starts over again. Jonah was again given the same command to go and preach to Nineveh, but this time God was more explicit in the message. Jonah didn't have any improvisational freedom in his sermon; he had to say exactly what God told him to say. There were no flourishes, no clever illustrations. It was a simple pronouncement of God's judgment.

Miraculously, the message was incredibly effective. Jonah took three days to walk from one end of the city to the other preaching God's message. However, it only took one day for the message to take hold. At the end of that one day, every citizen in Nineveh had been cut to the core. The city was turning to God with all their might, even including their animals in their fast (Jonah 3:7-9).

When we are called to speak the Word of God, we might feel inadequate, afraid, or vulnerable as we do it. But the bowing of the mighty city of Nineveh reminds us that God's Word is living, active, and able to cut to the soul and spirit of humanity (Heb. 4:12). We can speak the Word of God confidently, not because we are great orators but because of the inherent power present in the gospel message of Jesus Christ.

Not only that, but we can preach the message of repentance with hope in our hearts, for the city of Nineveh repented from the least to the greatest, and God saw what they had done and relented of His judgment. He did the same thing with us when we repented and trusted in His grace through Jesus Christ. Thankfully, we know of this One better than Jonah.

Our story is that we were the enemies of God. God appointed another, Someone better than Jonah, to come and declare His message of repentance and forgiveness. This One bent Himself fully to the will of God, though it cost Him His life. He too was swallowed up for three days and three nights, not by a fish but by the grave. Then He emerged victorious. Jesus is the second and better Jonah, and we are the enemies who have been granted forgiveness because of Him.

How has God used discipline in your life to bring you in line with His will?

Put yourself in Jonah's place. How might your perspective have changed after being inside the great fish?

Does it surprise you that Jonah's simple message was so effective? Why or why not?

Personal Study 3

God reveals His compassion for a rebellious people and prophet.

Read Jonah 4:1-4,8-11.

It seems that Jonah's repentance didn't fully take hold of himself. He was in the fish; he repented; he faithfully preached the message; and what he thought would happen indeed happened. You've got to give it to Jonah—he was confident in the power of God's word and in the gracious character of God. But Jonah didn't respond to the revival that broke out the way we would expect him to. He was not overjoyed at seeing God's grace and mercy poured out. He was angry. We can picture Jonah standing with his arms crossed, rolling his eyes, as scores of Ninevites repented and cried out to God. He simply could not overcome his bias and hatred.

And so, once again, the pursuing God confronted His servant. Verse 4 is a rhetorical question in line with several others we encounter in Scripture:

• When Adam and Eve first sinned, God responded with the question "Where are you?" Then He asked Eve directly, "What is this you have done?" (Gen. 3:9,13).

• God responded to Job's accusations with a series of questions like "Where were you when I…?" (Job 38:4).

• Jesus asked the disciples, "Who do you say that I am?" (Matt. 16:15).

In all these questions, God wasn't seeking information He didn't already have. Instead, He was pressing His people into recognizing the true issues of their hearts.

Despite all that had happened in the previous few days of Jonah's life, he was still unwilling to confront his own heart issues. Like the Ninevites who were clinging to idols, Jonah was clinging to the idol of his own hatred. He simply couldn't let it go, and his refusal to do so revealed that though He intellectually recognized the magnitude of God's gracious compassion, he could not put it into practice himself.

Like Jonah, we must confront the long-held prejudice and hatred in our hearts that might cause us to withhold forgiveness and compassion from others. When we bear ill will toward others, we show that we have not truly understood and experienced the fullness of God's grace given to us.

The truth is Jonah was right. The Ninevites did deserve to be punished for their wickedness. Those sailors on the ship to Tarshish also deserved to be swallowed up by the sea for their idolatry. No doubt there are people in your life and in our culture who deserve the righteous judgment of God—just as we also do. But what Jonah missed was that he too deserved to be punished for his disobedience. He wanted to be a hoarder of God's grace. God's grace and compassion toward him, and his people, was a good thing, but these same acts of God going out to others was inconceivable, and we are often the same way.

We love the grace of God as long as it applies to us, but we become disgruntled with a God who loves our enemies. Yet these are precisely the people that we are meant to run toward. Still, it is easy for us to act as Jonah instead, emotionally distancing ourselves from the people whom God loves. Logically we know that we cannot hide from God and His mission, but that does not stop us from trying.

How did God's compassion expose Jonah's heart?

What people do you, right now, fail to view with compassion?

What does that failure show you about your own understanding of sin and forgiveness?

God's Uncompromising Judgment

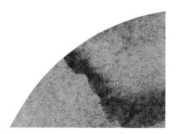

Introducing the Study

God's covenant with His people is not based on their good behavior or faithfulness but rather in His unchanging and steadfast love. Even when God's own people—or the rest of the nations, for that matter—persist in sin, God continues to seek after them to warn them of His coming judgment and urge them to return to Him.

> **How does the story of Jonah speak to our willingness to live on mission with God?**

God is patient, but His patience does not last forever. His kindness is meant to draw us to repentance, but make no mistake—God has promised that if any persist in rebellion, judgment will come. Just as God is bound by His own character to keep His promises of blessing, so also is He bound to keep His promises of judgment. As the story of God's people continued on, the patience of God ran thin and the promised judgment came.

 How should we as Christians rightly view the judgment of God?

Setting the Context

Through **His law** and through **His prophets**, God had warned His people over and over again of the consequences of abandoning their relationship with Him. Their faithlessness would bring God's judgment. God would raise up foreign leaders and armies to take what had been given to them by God—their land, their freedom, their prosperity, and even their temple.

Led by their kings, however, **the Northern Kingdom of Israel** was far too distracted by their idolatry to do what was right, as **"Kings of the Divided Kingdom"** (p. 35) shows, and God would eventually uphold His justice by scattering these ten tribes among the nations at the hand of the Assyrians.

 Why must we not neglect the holiness and justice of God?

Would **the Southern Kingdom of Judah** learn from their northern brothers? Tragically, the answer is no. King Josiah, the last bright spot among the final kings of Judah, tried every way he knew to return the people to their spiritual heritage. But after his death came a string of kings marked by idolatry and foolishness and eventually exile and destruction at the hand of the Babylonians. Yet even here, in this display of God's justice, we see how God preserved a remnant of people who would carry on the hope of His promise to make all things new through a coming Messiah.

> What are some ways you have learned or failed to learn from the mistakes and consequences of others?

✝ CHRIST Connection

God righteously punished His people for their sin, but He remained faithful to them and kept the promise He made to David to preserve a remnant and provide a king. Ultimately, God punished our sin through His Son, Jesus, and made Him our King forever.

Kings *of the* Divided Kingdom

In the Lord's Eyes...

	Did What Was Right Like David	Did What Was Right but Not Like David	Did What Was Evil	Did What Was Evil, but More Than Others
The Northern Kingdom of Israel		Jehu (but followed in the sins of Jeroboam)	Jeroboam, Nadab, Baasha, Elah, Zimri, Ahaziah, Joram, Jehoahaz, Jehoash, Jeroboam II, Zechariah, Shallum, Menahem, Pekahiah, Pekah, Hoshea	Omri, Ahab
The Southern Kingdom of Judah	Asa, Jehoshaphat, Hezekiah, Josiah	Joash, Amaziah, Uzziah, Jotham	Rehoboam, Abijam, Jehoram, Ahaziah, Ahaz, Jehoahaz, Jehoiakim, Jehoiachin, Zedekiah	Manasseh, Amon

Continuing the Discussion

 Watch this session's video, and then continue the group discussion using the following guide.

Why do you think we tend to doubt the reality of God's judgment?

What are some of the broad lessons we can learn from the fall of Israel and Judah?

As a group, read 2 Kings 17:6-13.

✳ What can you learn about the character of God from these verses?

What are some gods our hearts can drift toward, and what are some ways we can prevent this?

How should the good news that God accepts us because of Christ's work give us a passionate affection for God more powerful than for any idol?

The day had finally come. As God said He would, He raised up the Assyrian Empire to destroy the Northern Kingdom of Israel. God's people were judged for their consistent and unrelenting idolatry. But even in that judgment, God was faithful to maintain a remnant of the people He had called by His name. They were deported, but they continued on.

As a group, read 2 Chronicles 36:11-16.

How would you describe the character of Zedekiah?

In what ways might we ridicule God's message today?

✳ Why is pride so destructive in the lives of God's people?

As the last king of the Southern Kingdom of Judah, Zedekiah embodied the characteristics that brought judgment on the people. His pride, rebellion, and hardness of heart were indicative of the people he ruled. The people of God had forgotten the God who had been so faithful, and they turned away from Him.

As a group, read 2 Chronicles 36:17-21.

Why was the destruction of God's temple so devastating for the people?

Put yourself in the place of those people taken into exile. What are some of the things you might have been thinking?

✳ Where do you see hope in these verses, even in the midst of judgment?

Perhaps the greatest tragedy of the fall of Judah was that the temple, the symbol of God's presence among His people, was destroyed. Surely many in Judah wondered if God had abandoned them. Yet God left His faithful witness, Jeremiah, among the people to remind them yet again of His faithful love. He had not abandoned them. Rescue would come.

✞ MISSIONAL Application

Record in this space at least one way you will apply the truth of Scripture as one who recognizes the holiness and justice of God and has experienced His mercy and grace.

Personal Study 1

Faithlessness leads to idolatry and a fall.

Read 2 Kings 17:6-13.

Amnesia is a condition in which one's memory is lost. There are many types of amnesia. Anterograde amnesia is the loss of short-term memory while retrograde amnesia is the loss of most or all memories before its onset. There is post-traumatic amnesia, dissociative amnesia, and even lacunar amnesia, the loss of memory concerning a specific event or experience. But God's people suffered a different form—a spiritual amnesia.

Throughout the Old Testament, God constantly called His people to remember. In Joshua 4:1-7, God told Joshua to instruct the twelve tribes of Israel to place stones in the middle of the Jordan and on the land so future generations might forever remember what God accomplished at that location. Before the Israelites entered the promised land, Moses was very clear about how and what they were to remember. He told them to "be careful not to forget the LORD who brought [them] out of the land of Egypt, out of the place of slavery" (Deut. 6:12). If anyone knew how prone to spiritual amnesia God's people were, surely it was Moses. So he encouraged them to pay attention to their history so that in the future they would not repeat the mistakes they had committed in the past.

For many generations, the Israelites chose not to listen to the Lord. So in 722 BC, the Lord sent the Assyrians, ruthless and cruel, and they burned down the cities in the Northern Kingdom and took the people as their prisoners. Because of their disobedience, God's people learned the hard way that God meant what He said in Exodus 20:4-5: "Do not make an idol for yourself, whether in the shape of anything in the heavens above or on the earth below or in the waters under the earth. Do not bow in worship to them, and do not serve them; for I, the LORD your God, am a jealous God, punishing the children for the fathers' iniquity, to the third and fourth generations of those who hate me."

Because the Israelites returned time and time again to the worship of Baal, God disciplined the nation He had set His affection on. Because they had broken their allegiance to the Lord and had practiced pagan worship rituals, God drew them back to Himself through the use of foreign armies.

The psalmist said, "I will remember the LORD's works; yes, I will remember your ancient wonders. I will reflect on all you have done and meditate on your actions" (Ps. 77:11-12). Have you ever equated memory with worship? Memory can be worshipful when we, like the psalmist, remember the mighty acts that God has accomplished. When we remember God's acts, we remember His faithfulness. When we remember His faithfulness, we remember the greatest act of faithfulness in history—Jesus Christ gave His life so we can forever bask in the eternal presence of God.

Jesus knew that we would suffer from spiritual amnesia too, and that's why He gave us a tangible reminder: "And he took bread, gave thanks, broke it, gave it to them, and said, 'This is my body, which is given for you. Do this in remembrance of me.'" (Luke 22:19).

In what ways does God's work in the past influence your walk with Him today?

What effects does one generation have on the next? What traits are we passing down to future generations of believers?

How does our distinctiveness aid us in our mission as God's people?

Personal Study 2

Hardness of heart leads to idolatry and a fall.

Read 2 Chronicles 36:11-16.

The Northern Kingdom of Israel had fallen, and Judah would later follow. Power shifted for several years between Egypt and Babylon, and so did the allegiances of the various kings of Judah. Kings came and went, few with any integrity, until Zedekiah was installed on the throne by the Babylonians. He was intended to be a puppet ruler, but he was weak-willed. Eventually Zedekiah succumbed to the nationalism of Judah and listened to the advisors around him who told him he could indeed rebel against Nebuchadnezzar, the ruler of mighty Babylon. Zedekiah, however, was not acting out of a sense of national pride or noble desire for independence; instead, he was living out the natural way of his hardened heart.

All spiritual downfalls begin as a progression rather than a free fall. And the first step of descent is hardness of heart to the will of God. In the hardness of Zedekiah's heart, we can see some of the warning signs that might alert us—and should have alerted him—to our own hearts potentially growing hard to God's will.

One of the sure signs of a hardening of one's heart is pride. This king never believed that judgment would come, that his actions would actually have consequences. Zedekiah "did not humble himself before the prophet Jeremiah at the LORD's command" (v. 12). Similarly, we might find ourselves in a pattern of behavior that because it's gone on for so long, we think it has no consequence. "Sure," we might tell ourselves, "I know what happened to so-and-so, but that will never happen to me." When our hearts begin to harden, we forge a suit of false armor, tricking ourselves into believing in our own righteousness, that we are too big to fail.

Lack of repentance walks hand in hand with pride. Zedekiah had every opportunity to return to the Lord, the definition of *repentance*. He could have listened to the counsel of Jeremiah, humbly acknowledged the word of the Lord, and demonstrated that acknowledgment by turning away from his own wisdom and coming back to the Lord. But Zedekiah was convinced his way was right, and because it was, he had no need to turn away from it.

We face the same temptation. We might acknowledge sin, even feel remorse, yet not take active steps to turn from it. Those who are unwilling to repent are those whose hearts have grown hard to the things of God.

We see one other sign of hardness of heart in Zedekiah—it was his lack of distinction between his people and the rest of the nations. From its very inception, God planned that the people of Israel would be a people of distinction on the earth. They alone would shine forth His glory as a kingdom of priests set apart specifically for the Lord. But in the days of Zedekiah, "All the leaders of the priests and the people multiplied their unfaithful deeds, imitating all the detestable practices of the nations" (v. 14). In other words, they abandoned their distinction as God's people and instead began to follow the ways of everyone around them.

As Christians, we should take a good look at our lives. Does your life look any different than those who don't claim the name of Jesus Christ? Is there anything distinct in your behavior that marks you as one of the people of God? If not, then beware. Take the temperature of your heart, for it might be growing dangerously cold.

How would you define *hardness of heart*?

What is the relationship between pride and hardness of heart?

Why is our behavior a checkpoint for hardness of heart?

Personal Study 3

Idolatry leads to God's discipline.

Read 2 Chronicles 36:17-21.

God's prophet Jeremiah bore witness to the downfall of Judah, and he embodied the heart of the Lord. Time and time again, even up to the end with Zedekiah, Jeremiah offered an escape from the wrath of God. He repeatedly called for the people to return to the Lord until it was too late.

God raised up Nebuchadnezzar, king of Babylon, to destroy Jerusalem, including the temple, and carry the people off in captivity. Judgment, long warned of by God and His prophets and yet never truly believed by the people, had come. The marks that had distinguished God's people as His own—their land, their temple, their freedom—had all been taken away. God had shown His love for centuries, and now He was also making good on His promise of judgment and wrath.

When we, like the children of Israel, persist in sin and disobedience, we should not expect God to shrug His shoulders casually and act like nothing is wrong. He loves us too much for that, and His holiness is too great for that. God will discipline His children for their disobedience. Though no discipline is pleasant, we should recognize the discipline of the Lord for what it is—yet another act of love on behalf of His children. God loves us too much to allow us to go our own way, and His discipline is evidence of that love.

The spiritual downfall of the people had brought about the wrath of God. Even so, Jeremiah's tears stand as a reminder that God takes no pleasure in exercising His righteous judgment. In the New Testament, Peter reminds us: "Dear friends, don't overlook this one fact: With the Lord one day is like a thousand years, and a thousand years like one day. The Lord does not delay his promise, as some understand delay, but is patient with you, not wanting any to perish but all to come to repentance" (2 Pet. 3:8-9).

The people of Judah never thought the end would come. Day after day, life went on as normal. The voices of the prophets, constantly warning about the judgment of God, faded into the background. Similarly, people during Peter's day looked around at their lives and failed to see evidence of God's judgment. Though Peter promised that Jesus would return, the people of his day saw no evidence of that second coming and continued to live as if it would never happen.

So today, Christians herald the consummation of the new kingdom along with the new heavens and new earth. We warn that eventually the end will come, and we live in light of the inevitable return of Jesus. And yet, there are still those who, based on circumstantial evidence, claim there is no God and certainly no grand plan to judge the earth in righteousness. But God's judgment did come upon Israel. And Jesus will return. And on that day, God will judge the earth.

How should it motivate us to know that God desires none to perish?

How does God's love frame the way we see and understand His judgment?

In what ways should believers today be like Jeremiah, weeping over the state of our world while delivering God's message to the people?

God's Enduring Hope

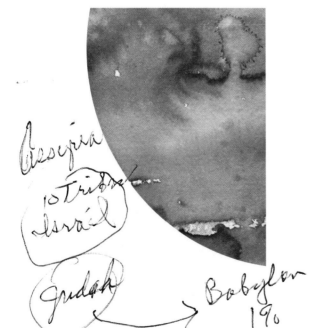
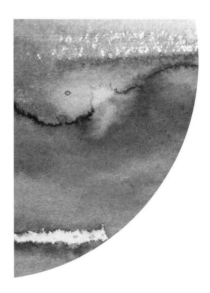

Introducing the Study

God keeps His promises. He kept them to Noah, Abraham, Moses, David, and to the nation of Israel. For centuries, God was faithful to bless those who blessed the people and to curse those who cursed them. But He was also faithful to His promise to execute judgment on His people as a result of their idolatry. The once great people of God were conquered and then deported, now strangers in a foreign land.

> **What are some of the questions you might have asked God if you were one of those taken into exile?**

The people must have wondered if God had abandoned them. Were all His promises now void? But even in Israel's darkest hour, God wanted them to live with a sense of hope for the future. Though they were exiles, God had not abandoned His plan for them and for the world. In fact, this exile paved the way for God's message about their true enduring hope in the future. God would initiate a new covenant with His people—one in which His law would be written on their hearts.

> ✱ **What do you think it means to have God's law written on your heart?**

Deuteronomy 29:29

Psalm 52

Isaiah - 53

Jeremiah - 31:31-34

Setting the Context

The days were dark for the people of God. The Northern Kingdom of Israel had fallen to the Assyrians, and the Babylonians conquered the Southern Kingdom of Judah. The land God promised to Abraham and his descendants had been taken over by foreign armies, and many of the surviving Israelites had been taken into **captivity**.

 How might circumstances like this have influenced the way you thought about hope for the future?

Prior to their exile, God raised up the prophet **Isaiah** to warn Judah and Jerusalem to repent. He spoke about their coming destruction, making sure through his prophecies that the people understood that the pagan kings would be instruments of God's judgment, though they neither knew nor acknowledged the God of Israel. But even in these warnings, the Book of Isaiah contains some of the most vivid messages of hope in all of the Scriptures—messages regarding the Messiah, God's chosen Deliverer.

Another prophet, **Jeremiah**, also warned the people to return to God. Jeremiah bore witness to the destruction of Jerusalem, but his prophecies also told of a hope and a future God had planned for His people—**"The New Covenant"** (p. 47). But with both Isaiah and Jeremiah, the deliverance and salvation of the people was something different than they expected. Their Deliverer would not be political but spiritual, and their salvation would be a rescue from slavery to sin and death.

What kind of message would you most want to hear from God in the context of exile?

✝ CHRIST Connection

God's people had God's law but were still unable to obey Him due to the sinfulness of their hearts. Isaiah and Jeremiah prophesied about a coming day when God would forgive His people's sins and write His law on their hearts. These prophecies point to God's provision of Jesus. Through Jesus, God offers us forgiveness, and through the Holy Spirit, God enables us to obey His commands.

The New Covenant

COVENANTS OF SCRIPTURE	RECIPIENTS	COMMANDS	PROMISES/ CONDITIONS
Abrahamic Covenant (Genesis 12; 15; 17) **Permanent Covenant** (Genesis 17:7)	Abraham, Isaac, and Jacob and their descendants	• Keep the covenant • Circumcise every male	• Land • Offspring • Blessing
Mosaic (Old) Covenant (Exodus 19–24) *Moses*	The people of Israel	• Keep the covenant • Obey the law	• Blessing for obedience • Curse for disobedience
Davidic Covenant (2 Samuel 7; Psalm 89) **Permanent Covenant** (2 Sam. 23:5) *Jesus*	David and his descendants	• Keep the covenant • Obey the law	• A great name • Stability for God's people with an eternal house, kingdom, and throne
New Covenant (Jeremiah 31:31-34; Ezekiel 36–37) **Permanent Covenant** (Ezekiel 37:26)	Believers in the Messiah	• Keep the covenant • Repentance and faith	• A new heart indwelt by God's Holy Spirit • Cleansing and forgiveness of sin • A Davidic king forever

Covenants & Dispensation

Continuing the Discussion

▶ Watch this session's video, and then continue the group discussion using the following guide.

Why is it important to keep in view God's promises in general and especially during times of suffering?

What are some ways that the messages of Isaiah and Jeremiah remind us of God's faithfulness even during times of suffering?

As a group, read Isaiah 53:4-12.

What part of these verses stands out the most to you? Why?

✳ What are some of the ways you see the life and death of Jesus foreshadowed in this prophecy?

Why is it important for us to understand that this prophecy was written hundreds of years before the birth of Jesus?

Isaiah shared this prophecy approximately seven hundred years before the birth of Christ. In this, we are reminded that the coming of Christ to die and be raised again was not an afterthought to God. Rather, the gospel has been the center of God's plan all along. These verses show us that though Israel might have been looking for a political savior, God would provide them the greater Savior they truly needed.

As a group, read Jeremiah 31:8-14.

✳ Why might this prophecy have been so encouraging to God's people when they were in exile?

Why would it have been so meaningful for them to hear that God would return them to their land?

Both the Northern and Southern Kingdoms had been defeated and the people taken away as exiles. But both nations would find mercy by the grace of God, for God would one day restore them to their homeland. These verses are a picture of life going back to how it was always meant to be, and yet, they are only a shadow of the true restoration God is performing not just with Israel but also with the entire world through the gospel. One day, all will be as it was always meant to have been.

As a group, read Jeremiah 31:31-34.

How do these verses point us to our deepest need?

✳ Where do you see the gospel in this prophecy?

What are some of the main differences between the old covenant and the new covenant God promised in these verses?

God was going to do something new. His new covenant would solve our deepest need—the solution to our own sinful hearts. Though we might not realize it, our chief and most desperate problem is that our hearts are corrupted by sin. In this passage, God reveals that true need and promises that He Himself would provide the answer.

✝ MISSIONAL Application

Record in this space at least one way you will apply the truth of Scripture as a one who has been blessed by the new covenant of God in Jesus Christ.

Personal Study 1

God will provide a Suffering Servant for His people.

Read Isaiah 53:4-12.

The people must have wondered if there was any hope at all. They were beaten, dejected, and enslaved. And yet, they could still call to mind the prophecies from Isaiah who, though he had warned them of God's coming judgment, also pointed to a future day of God's restoration and deliverance. This restoration would come from the Messiah, God's Anointed One, and one of the most vivid descriptions of the Messiah is found in these verses.

Put yourself in the time of Isaiah's prophecy, listening to these words. Imagine your anticipation of a coming Messiah who would set captives free. What kind of Messiah would you expect? Maybe the promised One will stand ten feet tall, weighing in at four hundred and fifty pounds of solid muscle, the heavyweight champion of the world. With one swing of His sword, He could chop down a hundred men, take back all that had ever been stolen from Israel, slay every enemy great and small, repay every oppressor of His people with humiliation, and reign forevermore. That's what you'd expect, and it seems that is how the prophecy begins in Isaiah 52:13: the Servant will be high and lifted up and exalted!

But then, instead of hearing words like *king, power,* and *conquer,* you hear words like *grief, sorrow, stricken,* and *afflicted.* You start to understand that this Servant will be humbled before He is exalted, rejected before He is accepted. In the midst of prophesied enslavement, during the uncertainty, suffering, and oppression of God's people, the Messiah is promised. But instead of the heavyweight champion of the world that we all wanted, we got a disfigured suffering Servant, and we were repulsed by Him.

What made this Servant so repulsive to us? He bore griefs and carried sorrows. He was stricken, afflicted, pierced, and crushed. We were nauseated at the sight of a Savior who had wounds. After all, conquerors aren't supposed to be wounded; they are the ones who are supposed to be wounding others. But our repulsion runs even deeper than that. This Messiah didn't just bear any griefs and carry any sorrows—He carried ours. We are placed in a position we don't want to be in, forced to confront our sinfulness and need of a Savior.

In this passage, we see God's desired outcome (salvation for people) and the way it is accomplished (the death of the Servant). The victory of God is demonstrated in the righteous Servant justifying sinners. The beauty of a holy and loving God is on full display in the cross of Jesus Christ.

In this mysterious prophecy, we see a glimpse of Jesus accomplishing the victory of salvation through suffering. At the cross, God fully demonstrated His justice. Holding nothing back, He poured out His full wrath against our sin. At the cross, He fully demonstrated His mercy by sending His Son to die in our place, to take the punishment we deserve.

Isaiah 53 was written several hundred years before Jesus was born. How does the specific nature of these prophecies increase your confidence in God's Word?

What are some ways we can reflect the mercy and justice of God to unbelievers?

Why is it important that Christians be known for both justice and mercy? What happens when we focus on one to the exclusion of the other?

Personal Study 2

God will restore the land of His people.

Read Jeremiah 31:8-14.

God's people were in exile. The land God had promised to their forefathers, Abraham, Isaac, and Jacob, was now in the hands of the nations. The best and brightest of the Hebrews had been taken away from their homes. But God had not forgotten His promise to Abraham so many years ago. He would bring His people back, but it would not be immediate.

If you read the rest of the Book of Jeremiah, you find that God intended to leave His people in captivity for seventy years. It would be long enough that He told them, through His prophets, to marry, to work, and to seek the good of the land they were living in. All the while, God knew that eventually He would provide a way for the people to return from their exile. This would have given great hope to those Israelites who found themselves in faraway lands.

But it also gives us great hope today. It gives us hope because it reminds us that the promises of God are true and lasting because God is bound by His own character to keep His Word. Consider the great promise Paul would later record for the followers of Jesus in Romans 8:38-39: "For I am persuaded that neither death nor life, nor angels nor rulers, nor things present nor things to come, nor powers, nor height nor depth, nor any other created thing will be able to separate us from the love of God that is in Christ Jesus our Lord."

Why can nothing separate us from the love of God? It is not because we are holy, righteous, obedient, or even very lovable in and of ourselves. It is because God's promise to never leave us or forsake us is rooted in Himself—in His character, in His strength, and in His commitment. And thank goodness it is. God would return the people to the land not because they deserved it but because He promised that the land was theirs. And God always keeps His promises.

The people's return to the land also gives us hope because it reminds us that God does truly care for the here and now. One might argue that the issue of the land was of little importance to God because He only deals in matters of eternity. Sometimes we might slip into thinking that God pays little attention to our present circumstances. But our Father in heaven cares about things like our jobs, our homes, and our worries. He cares about today and tomorrow. We can, then, confidently cast our cares on Him.

Finally, the people's return to the land gives us hope because it reminds us that all who believe in Jesus have another land to go home to. In a sense, we are all strangers and aliens. When we put our trust in Jesus, we are adopted into God's family, and as such, we have a new home with Him. This world as it is now, even our bodies as they are now, are only temporary dwellings in which we reside, but our true home is elsewhere—the new heavens and the new earth.

As we read the description of what it would be like when the exiles were allowed to return to their land, we get but a shadow of what it will be like when all of us who are in Christ get to go to our true home. With unimaginable and inexpressible joy, we will all one day enter into our true home, and our Father will be there with open arms to welcome us.

Why is it important for Christians to have a vision of their true home with God forever?

How should knowing that God cares deeply about your everyday life influence the way you pray?

Personal Study 3

God will change the hearts of His people.

Read Jeremiah 31:31-34.

Jeremiah's message to God's people was good news, but it was not the news they wanted to hear. No doubt the people in Jeremiah's day wanted to hear a message about outward prosperity, of peace with the warring nations around them, of stability in their lives. Though the people perceived their greatest threat to be from their conquerors, Jeremiah revealed that what they really had to fear was far closer than that—it was the sin within their own hearts.

Jeremiah's message from the Lord might not have met the people's expectations in terms of the physical, but it cut straight to the heart of the matter. Because our problem is far worse than we dare to imagine, the message is better than we could have dreamed. This is the promise of the new covenant.

But just because it's new to us doesn't mean it's a brand new idea in the heart of God. Sometimes we have the tendency to think that God's Plan A was the garden, but once the first humans willfully chose to sin against Him, God had to go back to the drawing board. In this scenario, the new covenant, the gospel, came one day as God had the brilliant idea of sending Jesus into the world, as if Jesus were Plan B.

But this is not true. If it were true, it would mean that God is on some kind of progressive learning curve, that He made an error in judgment at the very beginning and was then forced to scramble to make up for His lack of foresight. But we know that Jesus' life, death, and resurrection has always been the centerpiece of history (1 Pet. 1:20-21).

God's plan was not new to God, but it was new to the people. For generations, the people had a history of trying and failing, trying and failing, never able to live up to the written code of the old covenant of God. God was merciful time and time again, pursuing them to bring them back to Himself, but even so, the old covenant only imposed the law. It did nothing to empower the people to keep it. But here in the new covenant, not only God would provide the knowledge of His will but He would also write it within the new hearts of His people. The law was moving from the external to the internal.

Many people think of believing the gospel as a choice between going to heaven and going to hell. They know they don't want to go to hell, so they choose to trust in Christ to be saved and live eternally in heaven instead.

While it's true that trusting in Christ for forgiveness and righteousness is indeed the only way to God, if that's all we think of when we think of the gospel, then we are falling far short of its implications. The gospel is the message that because our hearts are so corrupted by sin, we need a new heart that is turned toward God. We need a change within us.

And that's why this new covenant takes place where it does. It is not written on tablets or parchment but written on our new hearts. When we believe the message of the gospel, the old person we once were dies and we are spiritually resurrected with Christ. This new covenant meets us at our deepest need—a heart engraved with sin. It promises a new heart indwelt by God. And this new covenant gives us the amazing privilege of living in fellowship with our Creator. The new covenant includes the privilege of a heart that truly knows God.

Why is it important to know that the new covenant was new to the people but not new to God?

How does knowing that you have a new heart change the way you approach obedience?

God's Continued Strength

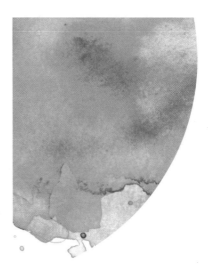

Introducing the Study

Even in the ruins, hope remained. Because of their idolatry, God's people found themselves living not in freedom in the land of God's provision but as strangers and aliens in a land of oppression. Despite these conditions, God's prophets promised that rescue would come, and although it was not the type of rescue or Rescuer they were looking for, they would nonetheless find hope in God's enduring promises and presence.

> **What kind of rescue and Rescuer do you think God's people desired when they were in captivity?**

Living in captivity brought all kinds of challenges to the people. Previously, they had been challenged to remain true to their God while occupying a land with foreign peoples. Now they were challenged to remain true to their faith in a foreign land with external pressure to conform. This is something we as Christians can relate to.

 Why is it important for Christians to know that this present world is not our true home?

Setting the Context

The prophet **Jeremiah** told the people that God had not abandoned them; in fact, he reminded them that God had plans for them, plans to give them a hope and a future (Jer. 29:11). But he also told them that their captivity would last seventy years. In this foreign land, they were to go about regular lives, building houses, planting gardens, getting married, and praying regularly that the land they were in would thrive.

 How do Jeremiah's words to the captives address our lives as sojourners in this world?

Some notable deported Hebrews, **Daniel and his friends**, chose not to cower in fear of the foreigners. These Hebrews excelled before both God and man, and they remained faithful to their God, even in the midst of great adversity. Therefore, God elevated them to important points of leadership in Babylon.

"Daniel's Life" (p. 59) recounts some ways these Hebrews demonstrated their faith. Shadrach, Meshach, and Abednego refused to bow to Nebuchadnezzar, the conqueror of Jerusalem, though it meant they would be thrown into a furnace of fire. Daniel bore witness to this, and his experience in seeing his friends' stand no doubt emboldened him for the specific challenge that would later come his way.

What are some of the ways you find yourself being challenged to adopt the values and priorities of the world right now?

CHRIST Connection

Daniel faithfully trusted and obeyed God even at risk of his life. God rescued Daniel from death and used him to advance His kingdom. Like Daniel, Jesus faithfully trusted and obeyed God, but unlike Daniel, Jesus was not spared from death. Jesus died and was resurrected to advance the kingdom of God.

Daniel's *Life*

REIGN OF NEBUCHADNEZZAR

- Daniel was exiled from Judah, taken to Babylon to serve in the king's palace (1:3-6)
- Chose not to defile himself with the king's meat and wine (1:8-16)
- Excelled in counseling the king in every matter of wisdom (1:19-20)
- Told and interpreted the king's dream by the wisdom of God (2:26-45)
- Promoted to ruler over the entire province of Babylon (2:48)
  – Shadrach, Meshach, and Abednego refused to worship the king's statue; thrown in the furnace but saved by God (3:8-30)
- Interpreted the king's dream regarding God's punishment for his pride (4:19-27)

REIGN OF BELSHAZZAR

- First Year: Daniel's vision of four beasts representing four kings of the earth (7:1-28)
- Third Year: Daniel's vision of a ram and a goat representing two kings (8:1-27)
- Called before the king and interpreted the handwriting on the wall (5:13-31)
- Promoted to third ruler in the kingdom (5:29)

REIGN OF DARIUS THE MEDE/ CYRUS THE PERSIAN

- First Year: Daniel received understanding about Jeremiah's 70 years of exile (9:1-27)
- Third Year: Daniel's vision of a glorious Man and the last days (10–12)
- Appointed as an administrator over the satraps of the kingdom (6:1-2)
- Ignored the king's edict and prayed to God; accused by his enemies (6:10-15)
- Thrown in the lions' den but saved by God (6:16-23)
- Told to go to his end and await his resurrection at the end of the days (12:13)

Continuing the Discussion

▶ Watch this session's video, and then continue the group discussion using the following guide.

Why do you think the temptation to compromise our commitment is so great during times of adversity?

How does the truth of the gospel give you strength to stand in the face of such trials?

As a group, read Daniel 6:6-15.

✳ How would you describe Daniel?

Does he remind you of any other person from Scripture?

What does it tell us about Daniel that these men were able to lay this trap for him?

Daniel's struggles in Babylon are not unlike Joseph's struggles in Egypt. Both men lived above reproach in their captivity, and others were constantly causing trouble for them or framing them. Here, Daniel was set up by jealous rulers hoping to cause him to fall. It is likely they did not want Daniel in charge because he was not corrupt and would not put up with their corruption either. Daniel's example teaches us what it looks like to live out our faith even in a place that may be hostile to it.

As a group, read Daniel 6:16-24.

How would you describe Darius?

✳ What must Daniel have believed to be true about God to remain faithful?

Much like Shadrach, Meshach, and Abednego, Daniel must have been confident in both God's power to save, and His wisdom to do what is ultimately right. One can almost imagine Daniel resigning himself to God's control, whether that meant life or death. This is the substance of true faith—not trusting in a specific outcome but in God who governs all outcomes rightly.

As a group, read Daniel 6:25-27.

> What is encouraging to you about the proclamation from the king?

✳ How does this proclamation reveal both God's mission and His glory?

God is powerful enough to use any person He chooses for good. Here, through a pagan king, God's purpose for His glory to go into the whole world is revealed. This is a reminder to us that no one can stand in the way of God and His purposes.

✝ MISSIONAL Application

Record in this space at least one way you will apply the truth of Scripture as a faithful stranger for Christ in this foreign land.

Personal Study 1

God's servant remains faithful even at great cost.

Read Daniel 6:6-15.

Daniel's rise in power was not because of his natural ability but because of the work of God and his walk with God. Daniel was a man who possessed the spiritual wisdom that comes from above (Jas. 3:17). And he was a man still bearing fruit for God in his old age (Ps. 92:12-15).

But as many have discovered, it can get lonely at the top. Success can increase your enemies. The blessings of the righteous can stir up the jealously of the wicked. Daniel not only possessed "an extraordinary spirit" but "he was trustworthy" (Dan. 6:3-4). But the envy and jealousy of the other officials led them to try to unseat Daniel, "trying to find a charge against [him] regarding the kingdom." They had only one problem: "They could find no charge or corruption … no negligence or corruption was found in him" (v. 4).

The only way for these officials to take down Daniel was to use his integrity against him. By manipulating Darius into making an irreversible decree, these enemies hoped to trap Daniel in an act of obedience to his God but disobedience to the king. Their goal was not to see Daniel demoted. Their goal was to see Daniel dead.

When Daniel was told that the document honoring Darius as the exclusive deity of the empire had been signed, what did he do? What he had always done. He obeyed God rather than man. He continued a pattern of spiritual devotion that had marked his life for years, a pattern his enemies knew very well (v. 10). Daniel did not take a month off. He did not push his religious practice into the shadows of privacy. He had honored God in this manner all of his life in Babylon, and he would not stop now, not for a month, not for a moment.

King Darius "was very displeased" at the situation and tried to find a way to deliver a man he obviously admired, appreciated, and respected (v. 14). Unfortunately, he had stepped into his own trap and he was caught. His evil administrators reminded him once more of the binding nature of the law of the Medes and Persians—it could not be changed (v. 15). When the king made a law, even he was bound by his words.

More importantly, these evil men had counted on Daniel to be true to his God. Daniel knew that past faithfulness would be no substitute for present faithfulness. Indeed, the past had simply prepared him for the present and the future. One's character is not forged in the moment of adversity but revealed in the moment of adversity.

Daniel knew what was potentially in store for him because of the edict, and yet, he remained faithful. This faithfulness provides a challenge to us as followers of Jesus today, a challenge that can be taken up day in and day out. We should not wait for a "lions' den" moment to show our faithfulness, just as Daniel did not. His willingness to stand in the face of adversity was not simply a moment of courage; instead, it was a consistent pattern he had chosen for himself. Day in and day out, Daniel was faithful in the small things, and when the moment of great testing came, he found that his faith and faithfulness had been exercised and had grown strong for that moment as well.

What statement did Daniel's refusal to obey the king's edict send to others?

What did this moment of adversity reveal about Daniel's faith?

What role do you think Daniel's consistent practice of prayer had in shaping him to be this kind of man?

Personal Study 2

God rescues His servant through His messenger.

Read Daniel 6:16-24.

This wasn't the first time God's people, living as foreigners in another land, had their convictions challenged. Daniel knew about his friends Shadrach, Meshach, and Abednego and their experience in the fiery furnace. Showing the same kind of backbone and conviction, Daniel did not falter in his faith either. Just as his friends had told King Nebuchadnezzar that their allegiance to God trumped every idol, Daniel demonstrated to Darius that his fidelity to God was not subject to edict, debate, or vote.

Much to his regret, Darius commanded that Daniel be thrown into the lions' den (v. 16). The den was probably a pit with an opening at the top. As Daniel was about to be thrown into the pit, the king spoke to Daniel, "May your God, whom you continually serve, rescue you!" Daniel, however, was not resting in the king's concern or his hope. He was resting in the providence and sovereignty of his God!

Daniel was cast into the lions' den, and "a stone was brought and placed over the mouth of the den" (v. 17). Apparently, this was to be sure the eighty-year-old man did not jump out! The king also sealed Daniel's tomb "with his own signet ring and with the signet rings of his nobles, so that nothing in regard to Daniel could be changed." We can only imagine the joy of these lords at this ceremony and signing.

Darius did not share in their delight. Verse 18 informs us "the king went to his palace and spent the night fasting. No diversions were brought to him, and he could not sleep." No doubt Darius' lords were out partying. Not so for the king. No food. No partying. No music. He knew he had been played, and it had cost him the life of his loyal friend, or so he thought.

King Darius went to the lions' den at the break of dawn expecting the den to have now become the tomb for whatever remained of Daniel's body. But Darius was in for a surprise. As Darius came near to the den of lions, "he cried out in anguish … 'Daniel, servant of the living God … has your God whom you serve continually been able to rescue you from the lions?'" (v. 20). Most likely, he did not expect to hear a thing other than the satisfied purring of lions following their supper.

Suddenly, and no doubt to his joyful surprise, Daniel spoke (vv. 21-22)! To paraphrase the conversation, we could imagine Daniel saying something like this:

"Good morning, my king. I hope things are going well with you and that you enjoyed a good night's sleep. I did! I slept like a little lamb with your lions as my guests. Their quiet purring put me right to sleep, and their warm bodies and fur kept me from being cold all night. Oh, I also had a very special guest show up. My God sent His angel to shut the lions' mouths. They have not harmed me, nor did they touch one gray hair on my head. Of course, you should know the reason. I honored my God and I never did anything wrong to you. I put the whole situation in the hands of my God, and this is what He did. I trusted Him either way, and I will continue to do so as long as I live. Now, would you like to come down and join me?"

Now, we should not take Daniel's deliverance as a promise that every faithful servant of Christ will be rescued physically from death. But what we can take to heart is that every faithful servant of Christ will be rescued eternally. That's because there was another faithful Servant of God who was also betrayed, but this Servant was not rescued from death. He remained faithful even to death on a cross, and in so doing, He provided the lasting rescue for all who trust in Him.

How did Daniel's dependence on God serve as a witness to King Darius?

How does this passage help you see the faithful way to respond to adversity?

Personal Study 3

God uses His servant to advance His kingdom.

Read Daniel 6:25-27.

Daniel was safe. Those who had brought accusations against him were punished, and God's justice was served, but God was not finished with Daniel yet. Following Daniel's deliverance from the lions' den, we see how God used this account to show His greatness to the pagan world. Darius was clearly impacted by God's miraculous deliverance of Daniel. In words reminiscent of the Psalms, and in particular Psalm 2, this unbelieving ruler wrote of the living God "to those of every people, nation, and language who live in all the earth" (Dan. 6:25).

The decree or letter began with words of blessing—"May your prosperity abound"— followed quickly by a command or warning—"that in all my royal dominion, people must tremble in fear before the God of Daniel" (vv. 25-26).

The declaration accomplished at least two important purposes: 1) it recognized the greatness, even the superiority, of Israel's God; and 2) it canceled out the previously irrevocable edict of Daniel 6:6-9. Once again we see the truth of Proverbs 21:1— "A king's heart is like channeled water in the Lord's hand: He directs it wherever he chooses."

God can even use unbelievers to proclaim His glory. The king's decree in Daniel 6:26-27 is a theological doxology that takes note of God's greatness universally (v. 26) and personally (v. 27). As to His nature, He is the living and eternal God. As to His sovereignty, His kingdom shall neither be destroyed nor brought to an end (v. 26). He is universally unparalleled and without rival. On the personal level, He is a delivering and rescuing God. He is not limited spatially, for He works His signs and wonders, His mighty and supernatural acts, "in the heavens and on the earth." In the most immediate context, just look to Daniel—God "rescued Daniel from the power of the lions" (v. 27).

Once again, God honored His faithful servant. Just as he blessed and honored Daniel under the Babylonian kings Nebuchadnezzar and Belshazzar, he did so again under the Medo-Persian king Darius (that is, Cyrus the Persian [v. 28]). The truth of James 4:10 rings forth: "Humble yourselves before the Lord, and he will exalt you."

And once again, God demonstrated His purposes to advance His glory through the whole world using His people. We can remember the days of Abraham when God promised to bless him. But we should be sure to note that Abraham, and his descendants, did not receive blessing just for themselves. They were not the destination of God's blessing but rather the conduit. They were blessed that they might be a blessing to others. God's intent with His blessings is that they go to His people, through His people, and that the very ends of the earth are eventually blessed.

Here, through the proclamation of King Darius, we get a slight foretaste of what is to come. Someday, when Jesus returns as the hero He truly is, representatives will gather around the throne of God to sing His praises. Jesus will be recognized as the source of salvation, and all glory and honor will be given to Him. In the meantime, we, as God's servants, have the privilege and responsibility of making that same proclamation in both word and deed until all the ends of the earth have heard.

How does our dependence on God for salvation lead us to mission in God's world?

What are some everyday opportunities in your life right now to pursue God's mission of taking the gospel to the ends of the earth?

God's Promised Restoration

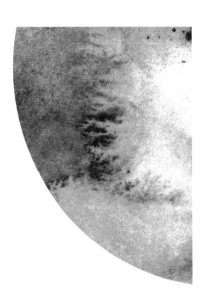
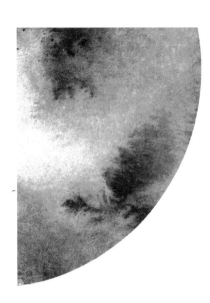

Introducing the Study

Daniel lived as an exile in a foreign land, but he remained committed to the purity of his faith even in the midst of opposition. He refused to compromise on the commands of His God, and God was faithful not only to deliver him from danger but also to use his faithfulness to advance His kingdom. The story of Daniel helps us, as strangers and aliens in the world, to see how to live in the world without adopting the values and priorities of the world.

 What are some ways the story of Daniel should encourage us to remain faithful as citizens of heaven in this world?

God is faithful to His Word. He was faithful to bring judgment on His people for their idolatry, and He would then be faithful to bring them out of exile and back to the land of their fathers. But even as they returned, their celebration would be mixed with sadness at the state of their homeland. As the people of God began to return home, the question remained as to how they would reclaim their identity as God's chosen people.

Can you share an example of restoration in your life, an occasion in which God has brought you back from difficulty or hardship?

Setting the Context

When the Southern Kingdom of Judah was destroyed by **the Babylonians** in 586 BC, some ten thousand Israelites were taken into captivity to settle into their new lives in Babylon. During those decades they discovered how they could remain faithful and worship the God of Israel even in the middle of Babylonian idolatry. For them, prayer and study of the word of the Lord became substitutes for the animal sacrifices that had once been their means of worship.

 How do the lives of the exiles in Babylon compare to the lives of Christians in the world today?

The Babylonians were conquered by **the Persians**. This new kingdom wanted their subjects to retain a sense of their own identity. To that end, **Cyrus**, the king, allowed the captives to return to their homeland and even rebuild the temple. So the Israelites made their journeys home to the promised land. Just as the Lord used the Babylonians to judge His people, He used Cyrus to begin their restoration. **"The Return of Jewish Exiles to Judah"** (p. 71) shows the paths the returning exiles took.

Among those who returned were **Ezra** the priest and **Nehemiah**. Ezra emphasized the need to return to the law of the Lord, while Nehemiah orchestrated the rebuilding of the walls of protection around Jerusalem. In both cases, it was the sovereign hand of God that not only allowed the exiles to return but also supplied the resources it would take to rebuild the temple and the walls. God was restoring His people.

What words or images come to mind when you hear the word *restoration*?

✝ CHRIST Connection

God brought the exiles back to the land, and faithful leaders rebuilt the temple for worship and the city walls for protection, but this would not be permanent. Through Jesus' death and resurrection, He made a way for His people to be protected from the enemies of sin and death and to worship in Spirit and truth forever.

The **Return** of Jewish Exiles to **Judah**

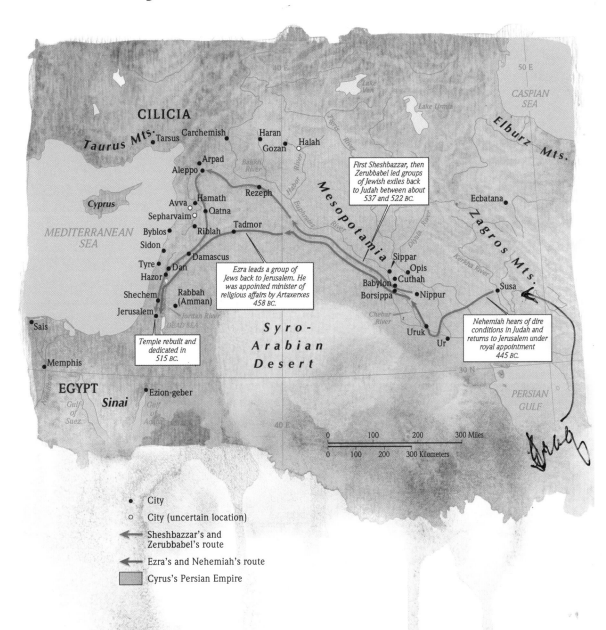

CILICIA

Taurus Mts.

Tarsus Carchemish Haran Halah
Gozan

Arpad
Aleppo

Rezeph

Avva Hamath
Sepharvaim Qatna
Byblos Riblah Tadmor
Sidon

Tyre Dan
Hazor Damascus

Shechem Rabbah
(Amman)
Jerusalem

Sais

Memphis

EGYPT Ezion-geber
Sinai

MEDITERRANEAN SEA

Cyprus

Lake Van

Lake Urmia

CASPIAN SEA

Elburz Mts.

Ecbatana

Zagros Mts.

Mesopotamia

Sippar
Opis
Babylon Cuthah
Borsippa Nippur

Uruk Ur

Susa

Syro-Arabian Desert

PERSIAN GULF

Gulf of Suez Gulf of Aqaba

Map annotations:

First Sheshbazzar, then Zerubbabel led groups of Jewish exiles back to Judah between about 537 and 522 BC.

Ezra leads a group of Jews back to Jerusalem. He was appointed minister of religious affairs by Artaxerxes 458 BC.

Nehemiah hears of dire conditions in Judah and returns to Jerusalem under royal appointment 445 BC.

Temple rebuilt and dedicated in 515 BC.

Legend:

- • City
- ○ City (uncertain location)
- ← Sheshbazzar's and Zerubbabel's route
- ← Ezra's and Nehemiah's route
- ▮ Cyrus's Persian Empire

0   100   200   300 Miles
0   100   200   300 Kilometers

Continuing the Discussion

 Watch this session's video, and then continue the group discussion using the following guide.

What were some of the specific challenges these exiles would have faced upon returning to their land?

How do you think their relationship to God changed as a result of the exile?

As a group, read Ezra 3:8-13; 5:1-2.

 Why would the reconstruction of the temple be such an important step in the people's return? What would it have meant to them?

Why was there a mixed reaction to the laying of the foundation of the new temple?

How have you experienced restoration bringing both joy and sadness at the same time?

The temple was the center of religious and spiritual life for Israel. The rebuilding of the temple and the altar in it was a priority for the people to reestablish their worship. In devoting themselves to rebuilding the temple, the people were demonstrating their desire for repentance of their idolatry, which had led to their exile. But as the foundation was laid, the reality hit home that this new temple would not be the grand structure of the past. The people were back in the land, but the land would never be the same.

As a group, read Nehemiah 2:17-18; 6:15-16.

What are some physical reasons why the rebuilding of the walls of Jerusalem was so significant?

✳ What are some spiritual reasons? How would the rebuilding of the walls contribute to the spiritual lives of the Israelites?

The walls of Jerusalem, which provided protection from the surrounding nations, had been broken down and the gates had been burned. For Nehemiah, this was an unacceptable state, and restoring the walls would be a powerful symbol of God's restoration because the physical state of the city mirrored the spiritual and emotional state of its inhabitants. Nehemiah and the people persevered by faith through opposition, and the walls were rebuilt. God's strength and protection of His people were once again on display.

As a group, read Nehemiah 8:1-6.

✳ How did the Jews respond to the reading of the law?

Why do you think they were willing to listen to the reading of the law for several hours?

Having completed the walls, the Israelites listened attentively to the law for six hours. In so doing, the people demonstrated they recognized that true restoration comes not in the physical but in the spiritual. Their failure to grasp this decades before was the reason for their exile, and this was what truly needed to be restored.

 ## MISSIONAL Application

Record in this space at least one way you will apply the truth of Scripture as one in whom God continues to work, build, and shape according to the image of His Son.

Personal Study 1

God's prophets lead the people to finish rebuilding the temple.

Read Ezra 3:8-13; 5:1-2.

The first six chapters of Ezra highlight God's sovereignty in the preservation of His people. God brought His chosen people, Israel, back to the land of promise. What's more, He used the ruler of the nation of Persia to accomplish His purposes! God Himself moved in the heart of Cyrus and the hearts of His people so that they could and would leave the land of exile and return to Jerusalem to rebuild the temple (1:5).

Consider the scene as these exiles returned to their land. The Lord had not been worshiped in Jerusalem for about fifty years, since the city's fall in 586 BC. So it's not surprising to see that the first concern of the community was to lift the Lord's name high, even though the temple had not yet been constructed.

The people gathered together, celebrated the commanded feasts and offered sacrifices as they were commanded to do in the law of Moses. The law gave God's people clear warnings against worshiping Him like the surrounding nations worshiped their gods. Deuteronomy 12:30-31 reads:

> Be careful not to be ensnared by their ways after they have been destroyed before you. Do not inquire about their gods, asking, "How did these nations worship their gods? I'll also do the same." You must not do the same to the Lord your God, because they practice every detestable act, which the Lord hates, for their gods. They even burn their sons and daughters in the fire to their gods.

One purpose of upholding the law was for Israel to be a community that stood in contrast to those surrounding them. The contrast was not intended to create an unhealthy distance from Israel's neighbors but rather to demonstrate the better way of the Lord. Though the people had recommitted themselves to worship, the temple was still broken down. And that was a problem.

The restoration of the temple was needed not merely for physical reasons but because of the spiritual implications of the structure. The temple was the lasting symbol of God's presence with His people, and in rebuilding it, the people were communicating clearly their desire to dwell with God and worship Him alone. The worship of God was meant to be at the center of the community of faith both then and now.

This is why the prophets Haggai and Zechariah led the people to finish rebuilding the temple, though it took them many years and what was new paled in comparison to what the temple once was. They did this because the prophets understood that worship of idols was what got the people into this mess, and worship of God was what was needed to move forward.

Like the Israelites, we can trace most anything in our lives to worship. Our sin, at its heart, is not merely about making a mistake or choosing a bad option; it's about who or what has captured the highest place in our affections. That is what we worship. We must, then, make it our business to ensure that we are fighting our spiritual apathy through rekindling our worship and desire for God alone.

What are some warning signs in your life that you are drifting in your worship?

What are some ways you can benefit the body of believers as you lead by serving or serve by leading?

Personal Study 2

God's servant leads the people to rebuild the city walls.

Read Nehemiah 2:17-18; 6:15-16.

The prophets Haggai and Zechariah returned with some people from the exile, and they led the restoration of God's temple, but there was still other work to be done. The remnant who returned to Jerusalem and Judah needed the comfort of God's protection as they inhabited a city with broken-down walls. And for a time, King Artaxerxes, prompted by the Jews' enemies, had prohibited the attempt to rebuild them (Ezra 4:7-23).

The report of the broken down walls reached Nehemiah, who was still in exile. He held an important position in the royal court as the cupbearer to the king, the one who handed the king his wine and made sure it was not poisoned by the king's enemies. Nehemiah set himself to prayer regarding the state of Jerusalem's walls and waited for the right opportunity to act. God moved the king to inquire of Nehemiah, his trusted aid, about what was troubling him, and Nehemiah was ready.

He requested that the king send him home, to the city where his ancestors were buried, so that he could help rebuild it. But then he pressed further. He also asked the king for authoritative letters to show the governors who had previously convinced Artaxerxes to stop the rebuilding of that very city. Even more, Nehemiah requested lumber from the king's forest to fund the project.

These were massive requests, and astonishingly, the king agreed. God had been preparing for the rebuilding of the land all along. As he had for Joseph and Daniel, God brought favor with kings, and Nehemiah set out on the journey home with an ambitious plan. It would certainly not be easy.

The construction alone would be difficult and arduous, but the people would also face opposition from those committed to holding back the project. The people were mocked, threatened, and extorted, but Nehemiah was sure of God's protection and provision in the task. He called on the people not to be afraid, to remember the Lord's awesome character, and to fight for the sake of their families and their homes.

Despite the threats from the outside, despite the threats from the inside, God worked in His people to accomplish His task in only fifty-two days! This is a clear reminder that God's people cannot underestimate what God can accomplish through them if they trust in Him and persevere in obedience.

Throughout this story, Nehemiah reminded the people that God was with them (2:8). He also declared that God would not only give them the ability to accomplish this task but that He would also make them prosper (2:12,20). Moreover, Nehemiah knew that God would not only frustrate their enemies but would also fight for His people (4:15,20). All of these truths climax in the triumphant declaration, even by their enemies, that God had accomplished this work.

But even in this great success we find the truth that walls of any sort provide temporary protection at best. No matter how secure the city, our homes, our bank accounts, or our insurance policies seem to be, they cannot protect us against our truest and lasting enemies—sin and death. The only protection from these enemies comes through the gospel, for it's only by the death and resurrection of Jesus that we can find true and lasting security.

When have you seen God do something so amazing that upon reflection you realized only God could have done it? What were the circumstances?

Why is it so tempting to trust in people or things other than Jesus for our protection?

Personal Study 3

God's priest leads the people to restore worship.

Read Nehemiah 8:1-6.

As we have journeyed through the history of Israel, we have seen how idolatry was at the root of their turning away from God. Because of their sin, God's people spent seventy years in exile. Now that many of the people had returned to Jerusalem, they were able to gather publicly and worship the Lord by listening to His word. This public reading by Ezra was timely. The law required the nation to gather together every seven years to hear the law of God read to them (Deut. 31:9-13).

As Christians, we do not have to wait for the availability of God's Word. We're blessed to hear God's Word proclaimed not every seven years but every seven days! The beauty of gathering together to hear a pastor rightly divide God's Word (2 Tim. 2:15; 4:2) is that we, God's people, are then equipped for every good work God has called us to do for His glory (Eph. 2:10; 4:11-16).

And yet, we live in a culture where it's sometimes hard to hold people's attention. In contrast, the people of Israel stood and listened to the reading of Scripture for about six hours! No cell phones, no social media, no electronic devices to fiddle with when they got bored. No comfortable seats. No air conditioning. No speaker system. They had been kept from hearing the public reading of Scripture for decades, but now God's voice was speaking again—they were hearing the actual words of God and they grasped the weightiness of the moment.

In Nehemiah 8:4-6, we get a firsthand look at how the leaders of Israel influenced the people by leading and learning. The people observed the nation's leaders as God's word was being read. Ezra praised God, and the people followed his example. The leaders in this scene were shaping their culture by humbly listening to God's word with the people they were leading.

The response of the people must have been an amazing sight. First, all the people stood when Ezra opened up the Scriptures. Ezra opened in prayer and declared praise to God, causing the people to raise their hands and proclaim, "Amen, Amen!"

Second, the people expected God to bless them through the reading of His word. This ushered in a sense of humility evidenced by the people bowing and placing their faces on the ground while worshiping the Lord. It's a beautiful sight to see when the people of God gather as one voice to declare praise to Him and to follow up by worshiping Him.

Third, note that they listened to God's word together. True biblical revival is experienced in community.

Why is gathering to hear God's Word so important for believers?

What things may be filling up your heart or life so as to prevent you from having a fresh hunger and thirst for God's Word?

God's Eternal Plan

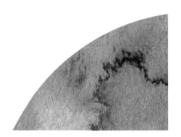
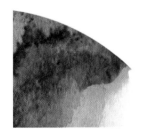
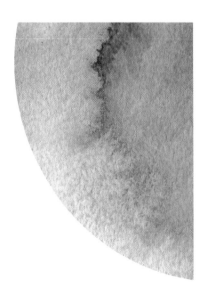

Introducing the Study

Just as the prophets foretold, the same God who brought judgment on His people through foreign rulers worked in the hearts of foreign rulers to allow them to come back to their homeland. Once they returned to Israel, their leaders led them to rebuild the temple and the walls around Jerusalem and to recommit themselves to the law of God they had abandoned over the years.

> Why would the people's recommitment to keeping the law ultimately fail?

While the people were aware of their sin that had led them into captivity, they would still be unable to keep the law they had committed themselves to. They were still living with old hearts, and they needed the new hearts promised in the new covenant. As time went on, the people indeed kept themselves from the idolatry of their past, but their hearts strayed from God in a different way. Shallow worship revealed that although they might have achieved a measure of external obedience, their hearts were still far from God.

 Why is it often easier to focus our attention on external behavior rather than the sin issue of the heart?

Setting the Context

The first order of business for the restoration of Jerusalem was the rebuilding of **the temple**. This was how it should have been, given the central place of worship in the lives of the people of God. Though there were delays, the new temple was completed in 515 BC. **Sacrifices** and **festivals** were resumed, and the people committed themselves to obeying the law. Things were going well. It seemed they had learned their lesson.

> What difficulties are prone to arise when things are going well in one's spiritual life? Why?

Sadly, within a few decades, the prophet **Malachi** had to deliver his message because the worship of the people had grown stale. He focused on the failure of the priests to fear God and to serve the people conscientiously during difficult times, but the priests mirrored the people—they all lacked the sincere worship God commanded.

The Book of Malachi is the last prophetic message from God before the close of the Old Testament. Then came **four hundred years of silence from God**. Malachi, like many prophets before him, gave the people a severe warning, but he also spoke of the hope to come. As **"Seeing Jesus in the Return from Exile"** (p. 83) shows, the Messiah was coming, and He was coming to deal with the true problem of humanity—the sin in our hearts. But would the people be ready for Him?

 Why is the gospel of Jesus the only solution for our true problem of the sin in our hearts?

✝ CHRIST Connection

After Malachi, the prophetic word of God went silent for four hundred years. But Malachi prophesied about a messenger who would prepare the way for the Messiah to bring God's kingdom. Centuries later, John the Baptist arrived as the messenger who prepared the way for Jesus. The last word of the Old Testament is "curse," a reminder of the consequence of our sin. But in the New Testament, one of the first words we hear from Jesus is "blessing." The One who bears our curse is the One who brings us blessing.

Seeing Jesus *in the* Return *from* Exile

Old Testament	New Testament
Cyrus the Persian Anointed by God to Rule and Rebuild the Temple (Isa. 44:24–45:7)	**Jesus the Messiah** Anointed by God to Rule— He Is the Temple (John 1:41; 2:21)
Zerubbabel A Descendant of Jehoiachin; Returned from the Exile (1 Chron. 3:17-19)	**Jesus Christ** A Descendant of Zerubbabel; the End of the Exile (Matt. 1:12-17)
Ezra Devoted Himself to Studying, Obeying, and Teaching the Law of the Lord (Ezra 7:10)	**Jesus** The Scriptures, Including the Law of the Lord, Testify About Him (John 5:39,46)
Nehemiah A Man of Prayer (Neh. 1:5-11; 2:4; 4:9; 5:19; 6:9,14; 13:14,22,29,31)	**Jesus** A Man of Prayer (Matt. 26:36-44; Luke 11:1-13; John 17; Rom. 8:34; Heb. 7:25)
The Sun of Righteousness Will Rise with Healing in Its Wings (Mal. 4:2)	**The Dawn** Jesus Will Visit Us and Guide Us into the Way of Peace (Luke 1:78-79)

Continuing the Discussion

▶ Watch this session's video, and then continue the group discussion using the following guide.

What does the people's return to vain worship after returning to the promised land teach us about sinful human nature?

How can Malachi's prophecy about the great and terrible day of the Lord serve as both a warning and an encouragement?

As a group, read Malachi 1:6-10.

What were some of the failures of the priests mentioned in this passage?

✱ How do those failures relate to the heart behind the act of worship?

Why are failures like these so offensive to the Lord?

God is the Father of His people, and He is a loving Father. But as a Father, He is also deserving of fear and honor expressed through worship. In Malachi's day, the people were bringing unqualified sacrifices to the Lord, the kind they would not even bring to the governor who ruled over Judah as a province. As an expression of love and devotion, true worship requires a wholehearted commitment. But the quality of their sacrifices revealed the condition of their hearts.

As a group, read Malachi 3:7-12.

In what sense were the people robbing God?

✱ Why do you think God cares so much about our finances? What do our finances reveal about our hearts?

Though the people had returned to the land, they also needed to return to God. Doing so would mean resuming the tithes and contributions. We should not make the mistake of thinking that God needs our money, nor should we think that being faithful with our finances will always bring material blessing. We can, however, trust that God will bless those in His own way who are faithful to Him. Money is the greatest window into our hearts. Jesus said that where our treasure is, that is where our heart is. This is why God cares so much about how we steward our finances— not because He needs our generosity but because we need to exhibit generosity.

As a group, read Malachi 4:1-6.

 Why is it fitting that the entire Old Testament closes with the threat of a curse?

Despite the curse, where do you see the shadow of the gospel in these verses?

The Old Testament is a story of a faithful God to an unfaithful people, and it closes with a reminder from God about the consequences of sin. But there is also the promise that soon another prophet would come who would pave the way not only for judgment but for the lasting change of heart that only God can bring. We will see that John the Baptist is the messenger who prepared the way for Jesus, who would bear the curse on our behalf and bring us God's blessing.

✝ MISSIONAL Application

Record in this space at least one way you will apply the truth of Scripture as someone who takes the worship of God seriously because of Jesus and the Holy Spirit.

Personal Study 1

Shallow worship trivializes God's greatness.

Read Malachi 1:6-10.

Given the pervasiveness of human sin and the hardness of the human heart, it is not surprising that the Israelites lacked "devotion," "passion," and "commitment" in the time of the prophet Malachi. But it still might surprise us to see this after all God had done for Israel. God had given His people the best: He had redeemed them from the Egyptians, led them through the desert, shown them the land, promised the basic necessities for life (i.e., milk and honey), marched them into the promised land, and conquered their enemies. And even after the people had experienced the consequences of their idolatry in the exile, God was gracious to return them to the land and provide for the rebuilding of the temple and Jerusalem. So part of us expects extravagant praise and loving obedience from them. Instead, they offered God what can only be described as worthless worship.

While the people Malachi wrote to may have been free from pagan idolatry or heretical doctrine, their worship had grown stale and lifeless. The word delivered to Malachi was a wake-up call to a people who were halfhearted in their worship of God.

Addressing His people as their spiritual Father, God handed down two indictments against His people at the beginning: they showed Him no honor, and they showed Him no fear. And not only did they not honor and fear Him, but they despised His name.

"Despising" means having an attitude of ongoing disrespect for someone or something. It refers to the act of conveying insignificance or worthlessness upon an object, idea, or individual. The text shows us that the people did this to God by offering crippled, lame, or blind animals to the Lord rather than the perfect, spotless sacrifices He commanded and deserved. He even asked them, "Do you think that if you gave the governor what you're giving Me that he'd be okay with it?" Of course not. God was so displeased with their worship that He wished they would just shut the temple doors (v. 10).

We could try to put this into perspective for a twenty-first century audience by saying: "Shut the doors to every church in the world. No more church buildings. No more meetings. It's over." But that analogy breaks down significantly because the Israelites were dependent upon the temple for everything.

The Israelites were dependent upon the temple for their sacrifices. They were dependent upon the temple for the forgiveness of their sins, for their festivals, for their feast days, and for their offerings. Without the temple, the nation would cease to function.

Because of how flippantly the priests (and consequently, the rest of Judah) treated Him, God's anger against them was kindled. This is not an image of an unjust, angry God. He was calling for the honor that is rightly due Him. It was the lack of respect from the people that ignited His anger against them because it minimized His worth. The greatness of God should drive us to our knees and cause us to give the absolute best of everything we have in adoration of Him.

The apostle Paul later instructed believers: "Present your bodies as a living sacrifice, holy and pleasing to God; this is your true worship" (Rom. 12:1). Peter shared the same notion by stating, "You yourselves, as living stones, a spiritual house, are being built to be a holy priesthood to offer spiritual sacrifices acceptable to God through Jesus Christ" (1 Pet. 2:5). In other words, the depth of our worship reveals the greatness of God in our minds and hearts.

What actions of the priests demonstrated their lack of respect and honor toward the Lord?

Are any of those actions or the attitudes behind them personally convicting to you? How so?

Personal Study 2

Shallow worship minimizes God's worth.

Read Malachi 3:7-12.

In the first portion of the Book of Malachi, God questioned the quality of the people's sacrifices. Next He questioned the quantity of their sacrifices.

Upon hearing from God, the Israelites demanded a roadmap for reconciliation with Him: "How can we return?" But their question was less than sincere. They were not expressing a desire to return to Him but denying that they ever left in the first place. After all, they were still sacrificing to Him, right?

Before we cast stones, we must remember how easy it is to wander ourselves. "Far from God?" a churchgoer might say, "I am not far from God! I go to church every week! My kids are in a Christian school. I abstain from certain practices. How can you say that I am far from God?" Yet many are blinded to the fact that they are blind.

God could reply to this in the same way He replied to the people of Judah: "You may not think you are far from Me, but you are." God had challenged the Israelites previously for their poor sacrifices, their lack of worship, their idolatry, and their faithlessness. But here He gets to the root of the problem: *the heart of the problem is a problem of the heart.* Specifically, they had misallocated their funds, choosing selfishly to keep and use what they had instead of honoring God with it. You see, giving is an indication of the state of our hearts and a measure for how much we value God's worth.

God actually told His people that they were to test Him in this. This is a remarkable concept—God said, "Try Me!" If the people would test Him financially, He would provide protection from those who sought to devour them, He would meet their physical needs, and He would prosper their reputation among the nations.

Trusting God financially demonstrates how worthy we believe God to be and reveals the level of our trust in Him. The quickest way to understand where somebody's heart lies is by looking at his or her bank account. Weekly giving is a visible display of trusting God on a regular basis. Where does your money go? How do you spend your time? What do you do with the things that have been entrusted to you?

We can learn three things from Malachi 3:7-12 about our actions and God's. First, as with much of Malachi, we learn that if we obey the mandates of God in humble and faithful service, we can expect God to act. This does not mean He rewards us immediately or even financially; however, when we trust God with our finances, we experience His blessing.

Second, we learn that what defines us is not what we have or think we have earned. Rather, it is what we do with the resources God has provided.

Third, we see in this passage that God is faithful to keep His covenant, even when the people are not. The people of Israel failed once again, but God never does. In the life of Christ, we meet One who gave generously of Himself out of obedience to His Father and, in His death, became the generous outpouring of heavenly blessing that God bestows on all who believe. God has blessed us to be a blessing to others. We respond by giving the Lord the best of our time, talents, and treasures.

How do our spending habits and our hearts relate to one another?

How should Christians understand and apply God's promise of blessing for obedience in light of what Christ has done for us?

Personal Study 3

Shallow worship deserves God's judgment.

Read Malachi 4:1-6.

Israel expected unending blessings because of their position as God's chosen people. What they received, however, was a warning. "Like a furnace," God would come to set all wrongs right, even if it began with them for their apathetic, lukewarm worship of Him. They looked forward to the day when the Lord would repay the wrongdoing of their enemies, but they did not realize that it would be a day of judgment for them too.

But we can be sure of our standing on that day because the Lord tells us in verse 2: "For you who fear my name, the sun of righteousness will rise with healing in its wings, and you will go out and playfully jump like calves from the stall." Those who fear the Lord, who have faith in His Son sacrificed for us, and who demonstrate their faith through obedience to God's commands—these people can look to that day with joy in their hearts, for they will be insulated from the impending destruction. "Remember the law," God said. "If you want to know what it is I want from you, then read it for yourself." Success is realized when we get into the Word of God and the Word gets into us.

The final two verses of Malachi are the ultimate cliffhanger to the Old Testament. The prophet ended with a promise of someone to come to herald the coming Day of the Lord and the warning of a curse if repentance did not have its way in the community and the family.

In light of these words, the people should have been asking themselves if they were truly ready for the promised Messiah to come. They had heard prophecy after prophecy of God's Anointed One who would bring true freedom and true blessing. Indeed, this Messiah would be the ultimate fulfillment of God's promise to bless all the nations of the earth through Abraham and his descendants.

We know from the New Testament that the herald, this "Elijah," was John the Baptist, who preached a message of repentance for the people of God (Matt. 17:10-12). The Messiah was coming, but would they be ready? They would have four hundred years to decide because the God of heaven was about to go silent.

For four centuries, this last warning of a curse would be left in the minds and hearts of God's people. The last word of the Old Testament is "curse," a reminder of the consequence of our sin. But in the New Testament, one of the first words we hear from Jesus is "blessing." The One who bears our curse is the One who brings us blessing.

Now, as the people of God, we would do well to recognize that Jesus is promised to come again. In that promise, the same conditions apply. We have been given the great blessing of God if we will repent and return to Him. But when Jesus comes again, the Lord will exact justice, and it is up to us to be prepared for it. The question we must ask ourselves is "Am I ready for this second coming?"

How would you instruct someone who sees the promise of judgment and responds by trying to get his or her life together? What is the proper biblical response?

In what ways does the Book of Malachi set the stage for the great coming of Jesus?

Tips for Leading a Small Group

Follow these guidelines to prepare for each group session.

Prayerfully Prepare

Review

Review the weekly material and group questions ahead of time.

Pray

Be intentional about praying for each person in the group. Ask the Holy Spirit to work through you and the group discussion as you point to Jesus each week through God's Word.

Minimize Distractions

Create a comfortable environment. If group members are uncomfortable, they'll be distracted and therefore not engaged in the group experience. Plan ahead by considering these details:

Seating

Temperature

Lighting

Food or Drink

Surrounding Noise

General Cleanliness

At best, thoughtfulness and hospitality show guests and group members they're welcome and valued in whatever environment you choose to gather. At worst, people may never notice your effort, but they're also not distracted. Do everything in your ability to help people focus on what's most important: connecting with God, with the Bible, and with one another.

Include Others

Your goal is to foster a community in which people are welcome just as they are but encouraged to grow spiritually. Always be aware of opportunities to include any people who visit the group and to invite new people to join your group. An inexpensive way to make first-time guests feel welcome or to invite someone to get involved is to give them their own copies of this Bible study book.

Encourage Discussion

A good small-group experience has the following characteristics.

Everyone Participates
Encourage everyone to ask questions, share responses, or read aloud.

No One Dominates—Not Even the Leader
Be sure that your time speaking as a leader takes up less than half of your time together as a group. Politely guide discussion if anyone dominates.

Nobody Is Rushed Through Questions
Don't feel that a moment of silence is a bad thing. People often need time to think about their responses to questions they've just heard or to gain courage to share what God is stirring in their hearts.

Input Is Affirmed and Followed Up
Make sure you point out something true or helpful in a response. Don't just move on. Build community with follow-up questions, asking how other people have experienced similar things or how a truth has shaped their understanding of God and the Scripture you're studying. People are less likely to speak up if they fear that you don't actually want to hear their answers or that you're looking for only a certain answer.

God and His Word Are Central
Opinions and experiences can be helpful, but God has given us the truth. Trust God's Word to be the authority and God's Spirit to work in people's lives. You can't change anyone, but God can. Continually point people to the Word and to active steps of faith.

How to Use the Leader Guide

Prepare to Lead

Each session of the Leader Guide is designed to be **torn out** so you, the leader, can have this front-and-back page with you as you lead your group through the session.

Watch the session teaching video and **read through the session content** with the Leader Guide tear-out in hand and notice how it supplements each section of the study.

Use the **Session Objective** in the Leader Guide to help focus your preparation and leadership in the group session.

Questions and Answers

✱ Questions in the session content with **this icon** have some sample answers provided in the Leader Guide, if needed, to help you jump-start the conversation or steer the conversation.

Setting the Context

This section of the session always has an **infographic** on the opposite page. The Leader Guide provides an activity to help your group members interact with the content communicated through the infographic.

MISSIONAL Application

The Leader Guide provides a **MISSIONAL Application statement** about how Christians should respond to the truth of God's Word. Read this statement to the group and then direct them to record in the blank space provided in their book at least one way they will respond on a personal level, remembering that all of Scripture points to the gospel of Jesus Christ.

Pray

Conclude each group session with a prayer. **A brief sample prayer** is provided at the end of each Leader Guide tear-out.

Session 1 · Leader Guide

Session Objective

Show that even though God's people have failed to love and obey Him repeatedly, God continues to pursue them, extend His faithful love to them, and advance His plan to purchase them from sin through Jesus.

Introducing the Study

Use these answers as needed for the question highlighted in this section.

- Though Saul looked the part of a good king, he was prideful, arrogant, and disobedient. Jesus is humble and obedient.
- David was a man after God's own heart, but he still succumbed to temptation and sin. Jesus is without sin.
- Solomon, the wisest man ever to live, abandoned his God-given wisdom and worshiped idols. Jesus is the very wisdom of God, given for our salvation.

Setting the Context

Use these answers as needed for the question highlighted in this section.

- Our true King is loving, gracious, patient, and just, everything anyone could hope for in a King, so we proclaim Him to the world.
- Though we were enemies of God, we have been saved by faith in Jesus, so out of gratitude, we take joy in serving Him in the gospel mission.
- Jesus never fails, and His mission will be accomplished, and we have the opportunity to join in on this already successful mission for the glory of God.

Use the following activity to help group members see the good news of the prophets.

Point out Hosea's connection to Jesus on **"Seeing Jesus in the Prophets"** (p. 11) and say that this prophet's message is the one we will be studying in this session. Then ask the following questions: "Why are the prophetic books some of the most overlooked books in Scripture?" "How can seeing the prophets' connections to the gospel and Jesus help to unlock the messages of these prophets for us?"

Read this paragraph to transition to the next part of the study.

The messages of the prophets may be difficult in the details, but they are simple in their intent: God wanted His people to repent of sin, be warned of coming judgment, hear again about His love, and live in light of hope. With this framework, it isn't hard to see how the prophets help to set up the coming of Jesus for the salvation of sinners.

Continuing the Discussion

Watch this session's video, and then as part of the group discussion, use these answers as needed for the questions highlighted in this section.

Hosea 1:2-9

- God has bound Himself to us as His people, even though we often act unfaithfully.
- We can prostitute ourselves with idols and gods of our own making.
- We repeatedly show our unfaithfulness to the God who has loved us and always been faithful to us.

Hosea 2:16-23

- True love seeks purity in the person and in the relationship.
- True love is forgiving and forever.
- True love brings peace and security.

Hosea 3:1-5

- Though we rightfully belong to God as His created image bearers, He paid the ransom for our sin to free us and bring us home with Him once again.
- Though we have turned away from God again and again, He continues to welcome us home when we repent and return to Him once more.
- The gospel makes us right with God by faith, but it also entails our sanctification, our eventual purity, by the work of the Holy Spirit.

Share the following statement with the group. Then direct them to record in the space provided in their book at least one way they will apply the truth of Scripture as a sinner saved by the ever-faithful love and grace of the Creator God.

✝ MISSIONAL Application

Because we have been purchased out of slavery to sin through Christ, we likewise pursue others with the good news about the God who pursues and loves us at great cost to Himself.

Close your group in prayer, praising God that He does not leave us in our disobedience but instead has paid the price for us to return to Him in purity.

Session 2 · Leader Guide

Session Objective

Show that God's love and compassion were not just for the people of Israel but also for the entire world, and use Jonah as a picture foreshadowing how the people would lose sight of this and wrongly believe salvation was only for themselves.

Introducing the Study

Use these answers as needed for the question highlighted in this section.

- We want vengeance upon our enemies, not God's blessings.
- It can seem unfair for wicked and evil people to be saved by God.
- We might be prejudiced against another people group or nation.

Setting the Context

Use these answers as needed for the question highlighted in this section.

- Whether we are among God's people or not, we should all be repenting of sin against God.
- Everyone exists as an image bearer of the Creator God, so everyone should repent of their sin.
- Apart from faith in Jesus, we all stand condemned before the holy God, so we face His judgment unless we repent and turn to Christ in faith.

Use the following activity to help group members see God's compassion toward the nations.

Call attention to **"God's Compassion Toward the Nations"** (p. 23). Ask group members to comment on the variety of people in this list to receive God's compassion (*a prostitute and a Gentile army commander; both men and women; individuals and an entire city*). Then ask the following questions: "What does this list have to say about our reservations regarding certain people, people groups, or nations receiving God's compassion?" "How have we already received the good news of God's compassion for the nations?"

Read this paragraph to transition to the next part of the study.

God's compassion toward the nations has been extended toward us in the gospel of Jesus, the availability of God's Word, and the loving fellowship of the church. Let us receive this compassion with gratitude and share it with all others with joy.

Continuing the Discussion

Watch this session's video, and then as part of the group discussion, use these answers as needed for the questions highlighted in this section.

Jonah 1:1-4,17

- Fear of the consequences, whether emotional, social, financial, or physical.
- We don't agree with God's decision.
- Obedience might upset too much the stability of our lives.

Jonah 2:10–3:5,10

- God can reach people who would seem hardened and antagonistic toward Him.
- God works through His people in order to draw the nations to Himself.
- Even a message of judgment from the Lord can humble a heart.

Jonah 4:1-4,8-11

- We should pray for hearts that reflect God's concern for the nations.
- We should pray for forgiveness for our prejudice and bias, as these are sinful in the eyes of God.
- We should pray for the nations to hear the gospel of Jesus Christ and believe God's Word for their own salvation.

Share the following statement with the group. Then direct them to record in the space provided in their book at least one way they will apply the truth of Scripture as a recipient of the grace and compassion of God through faith in Jesus Christ.

✝ MISSIONAL Application

Because we are recipients of God's mercy due to our rebellion, we put aside our prejudices and break down walls as we share the news with everyone that forgiveness is possible through repentance and faith in Christ.

Close your group in prayer, asking God to help you see the rest of the world with the same eyes of compassion that He has.

Session 3 · Leader Guide

Session Objective

Show that the people's rebellion culminated in open idolatry for which both nations were judged and taken into captivity. This marks a low point for God's people—out of the land again, but this time because of their sin. This session should convey the heaviness of God's judgment. In conclusion, hint at the hope that remains—the remnant would one day be restored, which leads to the final Old Testament sessions.

Introducing the Study

Use these answers as needed for the question highlighted in this section.

- The judgment of God should not be taken lightly; just look at Jesus' death on the cross.
- The judgment of God may seem slow in coming but only because God allows time for people to repent.
- The judgment of God will not fall on Christians because their judgment has already fallen upon Jesus, who died in our place.

Setting the Context

Use these answers as needed for the question highlighted in this section.

- To neglect God's holiness and justice is to ignore an aspect of who He is.
- If we do neglect these attributes of God, we will struggle to see the need for evangelism in this world.
- So we do not go the path of rejecting God in order to satisfy our own sinful desires.

Use the following activity to help group members see the need for God's King to come.

Point group members to **"Kings of the Divided Kingdom"** (p. 35). Allow them a moment to share any initial observations of the content on this page *(David is the benchmark for evaluating the kings; so few kings who did what was right; so many kings who did what was evil; the descendants of David in Judah were all over the place)*. Explain that Israel experienced several different dynasties of various lengths, but Judah's kings were all descendants of David. Then ask the following questions: "Does seeing the kings of Israel and Judah in this context surprise you? Why or why not?" "What does this evaluation of the kings and the resulting judgment on the nations have to teach us about leadership?" "What are your thoughts that the line of kings through Judah's history serves as the family tree for Jesus?"

Continuing the Discussion

Watch this session's video, and then as part of the group discussion, use these answers as needed for the questions highlighted in this section.

2 Kings 17:6-13

- God is faithful to His word, both for blessing and for judgment.
- God despises idolatry and disobedience.
- God is patient and compassionate, pleading with people to turn from their wicked ways.

2 Chronicles 36:11-16

- Pride leads us to think we can do things on our own and do them better than God.
- Pride in our hearts puts ourselves on the throne above God so that we glorify ourselves instead of Him.
- Pride takes our eyes off our mission to proclaim the good news of Jesus in the world.

2 Chronicles 36:17-21

- There were people who survived the judgment of God, albeit in the form of exile and servitude.
- There was fulfillment of God's word, which gave hope that His promises to Abraham and David could still be fulfilled.
- God promised an end to the exile after seventy years through the prophet Jeremiah.

Share the following statement with the group. Then direct them to record in the space provided in their book at least one way they will apply the truth of Scripture as one who recognizes the holiness and justice of God and has experienced His mercy and grace.

✝ MISSIONAL Application

Because we have been forgiven of our idolatry through Jesus, we listen to God's Word with softened hearts and proclaim His patience and righteousness to others while there is still time.

Close your group in prayer, asking God to give you courage to confront your own pride and idolatry and to call others to do the same.

Session 4 · Leader Guide

Session Objective

Show that even in Israel's darkest hour, God continued to shower them with hope, hope that God was going to provide them with a Suffering Servant who would pay for their sins and who would initiate a new covenant—one where God's law was put on their hearts.

Introducing the Study

Use these answers as needed for the question highlighted in this section.

- That we have a desire to obey God's law.
- That God's law has become a part of who we are and how we see the world.
- That we will share a close and personal relationship with the God of the law.

Setting the Context

Use these answers as needed for the question highlighted in this section.

- Captivity and exile could have killed any thought of hope for the future.
- These circumstances may have forced you to look for reasons to hope in the future.
- Exile would have felt like abandonment by God, which leads to no hope for the future.

Use the following activity to help group members see the biblical significance of the new covenant.

Ask group members to look over **"The New Covenant"** (p. 47) and to consider what a "permanent covenant" means. Furthermore, ask group members to discuss why the Mosaic covenant is not considered a "permanent covenant." Explain that a "permanent covenant" means God Himself will accomplish the fulfillment of this covenant and its implications will last for all eternity. The Mosaic covenant is unique in this list for its promise of a curse for disobedience.

Read this paragraph to transition to the next part of the study.

Each of these covenants points to Jesus Christ as its fulfillment: Jesus is the blessing and offspring of Abraham; Jesus is the Son of David on the eternal throne; and Jesus is the sacrifice that inaugurates the new covenant. And Jesus perfectly obeys the commands of the Mosaic covenant while simultaneously taking upon Himself the curse for our disobedience. This is the hope the whole world needs to hear.

Continuing the Discussion

Watch this session's video, and then as part of the group discussion, use these answers as needed for the questions highlighted in this section.

Isaiah 53:4-12

- Jesus was pierced for our rebellion (v. 5).
- Jesus was silent before His accusers (v. 7)
- Jesus was crucified as a criminal and buried in the borrowed tomb of Joseph of Arimathea, a rich man (v. 9).

Jeremiah 31:8-14

- It showed that God still claimed His people as His own.
- It spoke of God's comfort for His people in bringing them back to their land.
- The prophecy promised to turn their mourning into joy as God provided for all their needs.

Jeremiah 31:31-34

- God will change the hearts of His people with His teachings.
- This new covenant will be accomplished completely by God.
- The new covenant will deal fully and finally with the problem of sin.

Share the following statement with the group. Then direct them to record in the space provided in their book at least one way they will apply the truth of Scripture as one who has been blessed by the new covenant of God in Jesus Christ.

✛ MISSIONAL Application

Because we have been forgiven and have been given new hearts, we rely on the Holy Spirit as we obey God's commands and live on mission to make His kingdom known to all the world.

Close your group in prayer, thanking God for the sure and certain hope that we have in the gospel.

Session 5 · Leader Guide

Session Objective

Show that following God can at times come at great cost and that God is to be glorified and His kingdom advanced no matter what cost might be paid. God gives the strength to follow Him and to endure any hardship that might come our way because of our faithfulness to Him.

Introducing the Study

Use these answers as needed for the question highlighted in this section.

- So we won't be caught off guard by the struggles, temptations, and hardships associated with faithful living in this foreign land.
- So we can see the people around us as those enslaved to sin and Satan.
- So we don't get caught up in the trappings of this world that would distract us from the faith and our gospel mission.

Setting the Context

Use these answers as needed for the question highlighted in this section.

- We should live faithfully in this world but recognize that we are not of it.
- There are appropriate ways for us to live regular lives in this world, but we should retain our distinctiveness as the people of God.
- Our concerns for the well-being of others and for justice in the world are ways we can bless the world as descendants of Abraham through Jesus.

Use the following activity to help group members see how God's wisdom through God's people blesses the world, even when faithfulness leads to suffering.

Direct your group to look over **"Daniel's Life"** (p. 59) and to call out the familiar stories they see. Then ask the following questions:

- Why should the wisdom of God be considered valuable among God's people and for unbelievers? *(God's wisdom explains how the world should operate, and it provides supernatural information and direction for the blessing of the world. In other words, God's wisdom from God's people helps to fulfill His promise of blessing to the nations.)*

- What should we make of the dangers faced by these exiles because of their faithfulness to God? *(Living for the glory of God in a world that seeks its own glory will put Christians at odds with others, and this can lead to many painful consequences. But if the source of our faith is true, and He is, then standing for the name of Jesus no matter what make the most sense in this world.)*

Continuing the Discussion

Watch this session's video, and then as part of the group discussion, use these answers as needed for the questions highlighted in this section.

Daniel 6:6-15

- Daniel was faithful to his God.
- Daniel was persistent in his spiritual disciplines.
- Daniel sought the favor of God above concern for his own life.

Daniel 6:16-24

- That God's glory was more important than even his own life.
- That God exists and rewards those who seek him (Heb. 11:6).
- That God's will will be accomplished, regardless of how human beings plan and scheme.

Daniel 6:25-27

- God desires that His glory be known throughout the whole earth.
- God's people saved from sin for all eternity will include those from every people, nation, and language on the earth—a kingdom greater than all those on earth.
- God's people, miracles, and message all combine to show unbelievers that God alone is worthy of glory and He alone has the power to save.

Share the following statement with the group. Then direct them to record in the space provided in their book at least one way they will apply the truth of Scripture as a faithful stranger for Christ in this foreign land.

MISSIONAL Application

Because we are recipients of God's faithful love in Christ, we recognize there may be times when we are to obey God rather than the world's governments and engage in civil disobedience to advance the kingdom of God, even if that comes at great cost to us.

Close your group in prayer, praying for the wisdom and courage to stand faithfully and rightly for the name of Jesus even in hostile circumstances.

Session 6 · Leader Guide

Session Objective

Show that God brought His people back to the land out of exile and used various leaders to work together to rebuild the city to resume worship and prepare for the arrival of the Messiah. This session should drip with anticipation, though the people will slide back into sin once more.

Introducing the Study

Use these answers as needed for the question highlighted in this section.

- God honors the faithfulness of His children.
- God has the power to save His children from the hands of men, and even if He chooses not to, our resurrection is secure in Christ.
- Faithfulness to God in this world can display the glory and worth of God.

Setting the Context

Use these answers as needed for the question highlighted in this section.

- Our lives are sustained in the same way, through the provision of God's Word and communion with Him.
- While the consequences are often less severe, our faithful living in this world will invite problems into our lives from the culture around us.
- Like the exiles in Babylon, Christians live in a land that is not our home, longing for the coming of King Jesus to restore the creation.

Use the following activity to help group members see the significance of God's work in "the second exodus."

Call attention to **"The Return of Jewish Exiles to Judah"** (p. 71). Explain that sometimes this event is called "the second exodus" because of references by the prophets (see Isa. 11:10-16; Jer. 16:14-15; Mic. 7:14-20). Then ask the following questions: "What are similarities and differences between the first and second exodus?" "How might the return of the exiles compare to our lives as Christians?"

Read this paragraph to transition to the next part of the study.

The Lord used Cyrus to free His people to return home to worship Him. In fact, Isaiah 45 refers to Cyrus as the Lord's anointed. But though the people were being restored to the land, their restoration was incomplete. God had greater plans to accomplish, which included sending Jesus, His Anointed One, to save His people.

Continuing the Discussion

Watch this session's video, and then as part of the group discussion, use these answers as needed for the questions highlighted in this section.

Ezra 3:8-13; 5:1-2

- The reconstructed temple would have been a significant restoration of their worship of the one true God.
- It would have been big step toward a return to normalcy.
- It would have communicated to the people that God was present with them once more.

Nehemiah 2:17-18; 6:15-16

- The rebuilt walls would have comforted the people that God was with them once again.
- The walls would have ensured the safety of their worship of the one true God.
- The walls would give them faith that what God had torn down He had the power to rebuild.

Nehemiah 8:1-6

- The people listened attentively for six hours.
- The people stood up in reverence for the reading of God's law.
- The people bowed down and worshiped the Lord in response to His law.

Share the following statement with the group. Then direct them to record in the space provided in their book at least one way they will apply the truth of Scripture as one in whom God continues to work, build, and shape according to the image of His Son.

✝ MISSIONAL Application

Because Jesus has completed the work of salvation on our behalf and He continues to work in us, we join with others to complete the kingdom work God has given us.

Close your group in prayer, thanking God that our true protection comes not from physical walls but through the death and resurrection of Jesus.

Session 7 · Leader Guide

Session Objective

Show that the stage was all set for the arrival of the Messiah, but once again, God warned His people of their sin—now idolatry had been replaced with shallow worship. This session should be hopeful but also foreboding. The Messiah was coming, but would they be ready for Him? We will see in the Gospels that they would not be.

Introducing the Study

Use these answers as needed for the question highlighted in this section.

- External behavior is easier to see and modify to our satisfaction.
- The sin issue of the heart is beyond our ability to manage and change, so we focus on what we can deal with.
- The sin issue of the heart requires us to be much more vulnerable with God and others, so we choose not to go there.

Setting the Context

Use these answers as needed for the question highlighted in this section.

- Only the new birth through the gospel of Jesus can change our hearts.
- The power to change our hearts comes through Jesus' gift of the Holy Spirit given to those who believe in His name.
- Jesus' sacrifice on the cross and His resurrection defeated sin and death, so our solution to sin can only be found in Him.

Use the following activity to help group members see how God used the people during the return from exile to foreshadow the coming of His Son, Jesus Christ.

Direct your group to review the connections on **"Seeing Jesus in the Return from Exile"** (p. 83). Ask them to identify the connection that seems most unlikely compared with the others *(Cyrus the Persian)* and to discuss its significance for our worldview. Then ask the following questions:

- How was God keeping His promises in these connections? *(God promised to restore His people to the land after their exile; Zerubbabel is a continued fulfillment of God's promise to David that his descendant would have a forever throne.)*

- What are some ways you see the gospel foreshadowed in this part of the biblical storyline? *(The Davidic descendant is restored to Jerusalem, and his main concern is the right worship of the one true God; the law exposed the sin of the people upon their return and points forward to Jesus, the only One who can save from sin.)*

Continuing the Discussion

Watch this session's video, and then as part of the group discussion, use these answers as needed for the questions highlighted in this section.

Malachi 1:6-10

- Despising the Lord's name indicates a lack of fear and respect for the Creator God.
- Presenting defiled and unworthy sacrifices on the Lord's altar showed they did not take seriously the sin of the people, including their own sin.
- The priests modeled disrespect toward God in the eyes of the people instead of leading them to worship God with all their heart, thus rejecting the very purpose for their role in the community.

Malachi 3:7-12

- Where our treasure is, there our heart will be also (Matt. 6:21).
- The love of money is the root of all kinds of evil (1 Tim. 6:10).
- Whether hoarding money or demonstrating generosity, the way we use money shows how much the gospel has captivated our hearts.

Malachi 4:1-6

- The Old Testament points forward to the coming Christ but gives no power for keeping the law, so all stand condemned under the curse of the law.
- No one is able to stand as righteous before God, and only a curse awaits those who try to do so by keeping the law.
- The blessing of God comes not through the old covenant law but through the new covenant of grace established by Jesus in His death and resurrection.

Share the following statement with the group. Then direct them to record in the space provided in their book at least one way they will apply the truth of Scripture as someone who takes the worship of God seriously because of Jesus and the Holy Spirit.

✝ MISSIONAL Application

God calls us to take worship seriously, to magnify His great worth so that all people everywhere will know His name.

Close your group in prayer, asking God to make you aware of your own halfhearted worship and need for Jesus day by day.